THE
CARDINAL LAWS
OF FREEDOM

IKECHI AKURUNWA

i

Unless otherwise indicated, all Scripture quotations are taken from the New King James Version of the Bible.

Book Express Publishing House books may be ordered through booksellers or www.goexpresspublishing.com.

ISBN: 978-0-9729525-2-1 (Paperback)
ISBN 978-1-955495-03-5 (Hardback)
ISBN: 978-1-955495-02-8 (ebook)

First Printing
Printed in the United States of America
Print information available on the last page.
Library of Congress Control Number: 2021935879 (Paperback)
Library of Congress Control Number: 2021938113 (Hardback)

BOOK EXPRESS PUBLISHING HOUSE
Atlanta, Georgia
www.goexpressbulishing.com

DEDICATION

To the soul that wants to experience freedom.

CONTENTS

FOREWORD

I am delighted to write this foreword, not only because Dr. Ikechi Akurunwa has been a friend and dear brother in Christ for over eighteen years, but because I believe whole-heartedly in the lifesaving and behavior-altering lessons he eloquently expounded in *The Cardinal Laws of Freedom.* I also believe that it is impossible to find genuine freedom anywhere on earth outside The Lord Jesus Christ.

I first met Dr. Akurunwa in 2003. For the past 18 years, I have come to know him better. He is a man of integrity. He epitomizes Holy Spirit-instilled humility, candor, simplicity, and meekness, qualities that have become scarce commodities in these last days – even among Christians of every stripe – preachers included! He is a veterinarian and the author of many books, but more importantly, he is a devout and dedicated Christian. He does not glory in any of these accomplishments, for he would rather glory in the fact that he knows and conscientiously follows and serves his Lord, Savior, and Redeemer, Jesus Christ.

Many excellent books have been written based on the author's acquired knowledge of the subject matter and not on the author's convictions and deeply held beliefs as Dr. Akurunwa's. He writes from the depth of over forty-five years of walking with Christ and seeing the church metamorphose from one stage to the other. He firmly believes that everyone can experience total freedom by appropriating the power and grace made available to humankind by the redemptive work of Christ, which invariably leads to making daily wise decisions and choices in life. The reader is methodically taken through the divine pathway to being free and remaining free. In a nutshell, how to realize the seemingly elusive dream of walking daily in freedom is fully expounded in *The Cardinal Laws of Freedom.*

It's a book filled with perfect examples that are based on sound Scriptural facts and admonitions, which, if heeded, will certainly replicate the same results experienced by the repentant "prodigal son". If any would sincerely apply the truths and wisdom propounded in this book and is not changed for the better, all the hospitals and the best doctors in the world cannot help that individual. As he has poignantly and painstakingly delineated in these pages, spiritual problems cannot be solved by physical means.

The tone of this book is not preachy but compassionately instructive and advisory. The author is qualified to talk about the subject matter. He is not thumbing down on the reader; instead, he proffers numerous personal experiences to buttress his points. He practices what he preaches and empathizes with you, the reader, in whatever struggles you are currently experiencing. Yet, he does not compromise the Word of the Living God, which alone sets people free!

The Cardinal Laws of Freedom is a must-read. The book has ample lessons for everyone. To those who think they are standing, "Take heed lest you fall!" (I Corinthians 10:12); to those who are down, "Arise, shine, for your light has come, and the glory of the LORD rises upon you" (Isaiah 60:1); and for those who are seeking and searching, keep seeking, for "...the one who seeks finds..." (Mathew 7:8).

Emmanuel A. Enujioke, Ph.D.

THE
CARDINAL LAWS
OF FREEDOM

Ikechi Akurunwa

CHAPTER ONE

FREEDOM: WHAT IS IT ALL ABOUT?

*Freedom is not the right to do whatever you want,
but the will and the power to do what is right.*

Freedom is a highly cherished commodity. Sadly, not everyone has it. There is a cry for freedom from every mouth and every heart; from every street and every home; from every city and every country. No matter where you go, there are people behind prison walls built by their own hands, or by the cruel hands of sickness, or by the rusty chains of poverty, or by the strong arms of their governments, making freedom a challenging goal to attain.

What does freedom mean to you? Is it having the right to do whatever you want whenever you want? Or having the right to say whatever you want and to whomever you want? Or is it having the right to be treated with respect and dignity, regardless of your height, race, financial or educational status?

Some dictionaries define freedom as the state of not being imprisoned or enslaved. Of course, that's the desire of everyone. Nobody wants to be enslaved or have his or her rights taken away. No matter your definition, one thing is certain, freedom does not come cheap. In some countries, its road is fraught with danger and sometimes paved with the blood of the innocent.

The pursuit of freedom

The fight to be free starts in the mind. It starts by believing you are created to be free. The mind is where fear, unbelief, and deception can easily build their nests, and as you massage them and feed them, they will slowly grow until they fetter and incapacitate you. And until you flush them out of your mind, you will never believe that you are capable of being free. That is why as sweet and desirable as freedom is, some people have given up on its pursuit. They believe it's not something they can achieve or experience in their lifetime.

The good news is that there are still those who have not given up on its pursuit, those who wake up each day with a renewed zeal to continue the fight. In one of my poems titled *Freedom,* I expressed my sentiments about freedom thus:

Oh, freedom, freedom, freedom,
without you, life is sour and bitter,
yet when you freely fall
like raindrops into our open hands,
we quickly wipe you off
like something we abhor.

Without you, our cities are graveyards,
dark tombs gathering dirt,

pathways without sunlight,
fallow grounds, grey and empty vistas.

Without you, our homes are dark walls,
walls without songs and laughter
like the house of mourning;
like the face of a crooked day.

It does not surprise me
that sometimes you ignore us,
reject us, leave us in a lurch;
in the gulf of a smoldering fire,
or abandon us in a swamp, scary and deadly;
unmoved by our tears.

It does not surprise me
that sometimes you plug your ears
and go to sleep while we roast
or languish in captivity.

It does not surprise me
that sometimes you run away and hide,
leaving us to walk around with tearful eyes,
sniffing for your presence
and combing the earth for you.

But it does surprise me,
that sometimes you want to be
appeased with blood,
with tanks and warheads,
with gun salutes on battlefields

where the lives of our young ones
are shredded and littered on the soil
tainted with their blood.

It does surprise me
that sometimes you wait
until we turn our cities into shameful ruins,
destroying all we have toiled
and labored day and night to build,
watching indifferently as our children die
of hunger in our hands.

It does surprise me
that when your anger flares up
you do not segregate
between the young and the old,
you do not differentiate
between the innocent and the wicked.
You pour your wrath on all.

Oh, freedom, freedom, freedom,
why do you play the game
of tit for tat with mortals?
Why does your anger live
to see the dawn of another day
knowing we cannot live without you,
knowing our lives are worthless without you?

As enigmatic and elusive freedom may be, it is a road wise men and women travel every day. If you make freedom your daily destination, you will live a successful and rewarding life.

The footprints of freedom

Along every road of life are the footprints of freedom, carved by the hands of those who have fought and died for it. All through history, we read about heroes like Nelson Mandela, Rev. Martin Luther King Jnr, who, despite the loud drumbeats of racism in their ears and ceaseless harassments and imprisonments, defied all odds to engrave their names in the rank and file of great freedom fighters. They left us a big shoe to fill.

Despite all their sacrifices, the footprints of freedom are daily becoming blurry, covered with clouds of dust raised by endless wars between nations and races, or the rubbles from rivalries between the poor and the rich; or the turbulence caused by lands and seas revolting against humanity. But nothing can mask the road to freedom for anyone who is genuinely seeking it. Amid all the distractions of life, he will still see the bright light of freedom beckoning him. The sweet taste of freedom will remain the daily longing of his soul. He sees the footprints of freedom everywhere he goes and diligently follows them.

Trees litter their shadows and leaves on the ground as their footprints. Spiders litter cobwebs anywhere they can, as their footprints. Also, animals like coyotes, bobcats, and foxes leave remarkable tracks as they go by. With such tracks, hunters can easily trail them to their hiding places. In effect, footprints are unmistakable, including the footprints of freedom.

Among the footprints left by many great freedom fighters, none can compare with those left by Jesus Christ. He left the biggest and most significant footprints on earth. They are for humankind to follow. These footprints will take everyone who follows them to Calvary Cross, on the hills of Golgotha, where freedom was purchased for mankind through the shedding of the blood of Jesus.

Generational fight

Every generation fight for one type of freedom or another. Some generations fight to be free from poverty; some fight to be free from a killer disease; some fight to be free from corruption, and some fight to be free from the shackles of tyranny. The same is true of every individual. At certain seasons or stages of your life, you will face different challenges from what another person faces.

Suppose a generation does not have great spiritual leaders. In that case, that generation may be imprisoned by darkness with the grave consequences of endless and meaningless wars and divisions, hatred and wickedness, greed and corruption. In the same light, if a person is spiritually blind, his freedom could be easily snatched away from him by any dangerous arrow the devil jabs at him.

Sometimes, babies fight for their freedoms better than adults. For instance, a baby in a cot, every second that goes by, that baby longs to be free from the confines of that crib. As soon as he begins to crawl, he will wait for the right moment to escape from his prison. And from the moment he deems right, he will begin to make many audacious attempts to get out of the crib on his own accord. Sometimes, it may involve dashing his head on the floor as he climbs out of the seemingly secured and impossible height of his cradle. If a baby is willing to take such a risk to be free from the confines of a cot, an adult should be willing to do more to be free, even if it means climbing Mount

Everest. So, the beautiful garment of freedom cannot be won without a fight. But regardless of how fierce the battle may be, freedom is worth fighting for. If Jesus deemed it fit to die on the cross for your freedom and mine, then freedom is undoubtedly worth fighting and dying for.

Food for thought

- Freedom is not freedom without freedom. Partial freedom is no freedom. You are either free, or you are not.

- If you split the word freedom into two, you will have "free" and "dom" or dominion. So, to be free is to walk in dominion. Free people dominate things before they attempt to dominate them.

- Ten days of freedom is more rewarding than ten years in bondage or captivity.

- Those that fail to fight for their freedom today will always live to regret it.

- It's dangerous to sit in bondage for one day because it can lead to a lifetime of bondage.

- When freedom goes out of the door, so much goes with it, including your dignity and ability to chart the course of your destiny.

- When your freedom is stripped from you, or when you willingly relinquish it, you will become naked and defenseless like one exposed to harsh life elements and left to die slowly.

- Another day lived without freedom is another day denied of the opportunity to live a life without limits, a life of great possibilities and adventure.

- If you make freedom your daily destination, you will go further in life than most of your peers.

CHAPTER TWO

THE PRODIGAL SON

"Let it be known to you all, and to all the people of Israel, that by the name of Jesus Christ of Nazareth, whom you crucified, whom God raised from the dead, by Him this man stands here before you whole."
- Acts 4:10

In the African culture and many other parts of the world, names have deep meanings. Most African names tell the story of what the parents had been through before they had their children or are currently going through. If they went through a period of barrenness, they would call the child a name that either gives glory to God for answering their prayers or one that mocks the enemies who once laughed at them.

Regardless of your nationality, nobody would like to be given or called a bad name under normal circumstances. Yes, some gang members or comedians, or musicians proudly go with names that make the ears tingle. They do that simply because such names make them stand out in their business. Most times, such names also set them up for a great fall.

Luke 15:11-32 vividly tells us a story, the story of the prodigal son. Why does the Bible describe this son as prodigal? The word prodigal indicates profuse and wasteful nature; an extravagant lifestyle. The young man has a curious and interesting character that draws attention to the seven intriguing cardinal laws of freedom. For a clearer picture of these laws, let's take a closer look at what the Bible says about the prodigal son:

"¹¹Then He said: "A certain man had two sons. ¹²And the younger of them said to *his* father, 'Father, give me the portion of goods that falls *to me.*' So he divided to them *his* livelihood. ¹³And not many days after, the younger son gathered all together, journeyed to a far country, and there wasted his possessions with prodigal living. ¹⁴ But when he had spent all, there arose a severe famine in that land, and he began to be in want. ¹⁵Then he went and joined himself to a citizen of that country, and he sent him into his fields to feed swine. ¹⁶And he would gladly have filled his stomach with the pods that the swine ate, and no one gave him *anything.*

"¹⁷But when he came to himself, he said, 'How many of my father's hired servants have bread enough and to spare, and I perish with hunger! ¹⁸I will arise and go to my father and will say to him, "Father, I have sinned against heaven and before you, ¹⁹and I am no longer worthy to be called your son. Make me like one of your hired servants."'

"²⁰And he arose and came to his father. But when he was still a great way off, his father saw him and had compassion, and ran and fell on his neck and kissed him. ²¹And the son said to him, 'Father, I have sinned against heaven and in your sight, and am no longer worthy to be called your son.'

"²²But the father said to his servants, 'Bring out the best robe and put *it* on him, and put a ring on his hand and sandals on *his* feet. ²³And bring the fatted calf here and kill *it,* and let us eat and be merry; ²⁴for this my son was dead and is alive again; he was lost and is found.' And they began to be merry.

"²⁵Now his older son was in the field. And as he came and drew near to the house, he heard music and dancing. ²⁶So he called one of the servants and asked what these things meant. ²⁷And he said to him, 'Your brother has come, and because he has received him safe and sound, your father has killed the fatted calf.'

"²⁸But he was angry and would not go in. Therefore his father came out and pleaded with him. ²⁹So he answered and said to *his* father, 'Lo, these many years I have been serving you; I never transgressed your commandment at any time; and yet you never gave me a young goat, that I might make merry with my friends. ³⁰But as soon as this son of yours came, who has devoured your livelihood with harlots, you killed the fatted calf for him.'

"³¹And he said to him, 'Son, you are always with me, and all that I have is yours. ³²It was right that we should make merry and be glad, for your brother was dead and is alive again, and was lost and is found.'"

On the shelves of many public libraries and the archives of many decorated citadels of learning lie outstanding dissertations that have been written from the story of the prodigal son. Over the years, profound movies with great moral lessons have also come out of it, yet there is still more to learn from this young man's life. It's a story with great spiritual exposition about the futility of sacrificing family for self-gratification. It's a story that shows how easy it is to abuse grace; how foolish it is to trade things that have lasting and eternal values for worthless and temporary things. It's an exposition that unveils the utter darkness that lurks in the depths of an unregenerate heart. And more interestingly, it's a story that brings to light the inherent danger of breaking some of the laws of freedom.

Tucked in between the lines of the parable above are also the stories of our lives. Most times, we begin with rebellion and turning our back on God, then we embrace the world with its pomp and pageantry, and later we return crying like a child after we have been bruised and battered. We go through this vicious circle over and over again until we regain our senses and run to God for help, or we get stuck in our foolery until we get knocked down into an early grave.

Audacious young man

When I was a teenager, I was very shy. Growing up in Africa didn't make it any easier. At the time in question, most teenagers hardly talked when their parents were talking, much less making the type of demand the prodigal son made from his father. It was unthinkable to approach your father boldly and demand your inheritance. You will be a dead person even before you finish making the request.

The interesting thing about the prodigal son was that he was not even the first son. He was the second. He was the least qualified to make such a demand. My father had seven of us. I am the second child, but the first son. I don't know how I would have felt watching my immediate younger brother make such demands from my father. I would have probably looked at him and said, "What a greedy and selfish person you are!"

Obviously, the prodigal son's motive was questionable, and so are our motives when we make certain demands from God. Many times, we pray for a house we cannot afford or beg God to give us cars we very well know will drown our income. Sometimes we go as far as asking for permission to indulge in a lifestyle that is contrary to God's standards.

What is your motive for what you are asking God for? Is it to show off to your neighbors; or to announce to the world that you belong to a particular social class? A pastor once confessed to his church that there was a time he so badly wanted his church to grow simply because he wanted to prove to some other pastors that he was not at their level. This is a dangerous place to be. If your motive is not right, you are likely caught up in the prison walls of pride, or you are still a servant to your flesh, just like the prodigal son.

Family business

In every family, every child has his or her individual gifts and talents. There was no doubt that the prodigal son contributed immensely to the growth of his father's business through hard work. He probably did a few things better than his elder brother; he may have known how rich his father was. It could be he waited for the best season of the business to make his demand. With a bumper harvest, it was probably hard to refuse the request of a hard-working son. Maybe, he told his father he would replicate the business somewhere else to make it easier for his father to budge. Whatever his reason was, his father gave him his inheritance.

God sometimes allows us to have our way for a while to learn the lessons we need to learn. One way or the other, God has a way of pruning us to get rid of the garbage in our lives. Sometimes, He gives us that very house we so much prayed for when we knew our income was not enough to pay its monthly mortgage. He knows that after carrying such a heavy weight for a while, we will come running to say, "I am sorry, Lord; please can you take this cup of sorrow away from me?" There are always lessons to learn after a self-imposed trial. The sad thing though, is that we may never be in the position to live without the scars they inflicted on us.

Your inheritance

What have you done with your inheritance? Before you make any excuses, it's important to know that some natural endowments are greater than the inheritance of money from a wealthy father. What have you done with your natural talents and gifts? Some have wonderful singing voices but have done nothing with their voice; some have excellent writing skills but have tossed their pens into the attic; some have great painting skills and buried their paint brushes under the pile of a million excuses.

Everybody is gifted. There is something you can do better than others.

"11And He Himself gave some *to be* apostles, some prophets, some evangelists, and some pastors and teachers, 12for the equipping of the saints for the work of ministry, for the edifying of the body of Christ" (Ephesians 4:11-12).

Don't covet the gift of others. Use what you have to shape your destiny. You have enough inside of you to make a difference. The prodigal son chose to waste his inheritance. The truth is that it's easy to destroy than to build, a lesson many of us have learned too late, like the prodigal son. Maybe, the knowledge of the cardinal laws of freedom may have saved him a lot of pain. Let's take a closer look at these cardinal laws.

Food for thought

- What you don't value will not remain in your hands or life for too long. What you neglect will neglect you.

- You may never know how valuable freedom is until you lose it. How loosely or tightly you hold onto something is an indication of the value you have for it.

- Whatever preoccupies your mind for a long time is what you will eventually become unless you break from it.

- Your greatest asset can also be your greatest undoing if not constantly checked and channeled in the right direction.

- It's better to stay around people that act as checks and

balances in your life than to stay around people who allow you to do whatever you want.

CHAPTER THREE

THE FIRST CARDINAL LAW OF FREEDOM

The first cardinal law of freedom: *Your freedom largely depends on the choices you make each day.*

Being free from every shade of enslavement or bondage is a very beautiful life to live, but only those who know its secrets enjoy it. Only those who have found its pathway walk in it; only those who know its laws keep them; only those who know its value shield it daily from the arrows and gallows of men.

Choices

Freedom is a courageous lifestyle fabricated with the strong arm of truth and giving birth every day by making the right choices. It's the lifestyle that makes the right and hard choices of life whether anyone is watching you or not. Unfortunately, too many times, we slip and fall in the open from the rubbles of wrong choices we made in secret.

If you talk to some older people, within few minutes of the

conversation, you will discover that a good number of them have some regrets or others. They are quick to warn you to make sure you make the right choices at all times. At their age, it's probably too late for some of them to repair some broken bridges in their lives or to attempt to walk back certain decisions they made that cost them so much. Some of them wish they knew what they know today, and if given a second chance, most of them will quickly adopt a lifestyle of self-examination.

Why do you do what you do? What guides your daily decisions? What is the motive or purpose behind your actions? If we could stop for a moment to examine what we do and the possible consequences of our actions, we will be less prone to making wrong choices. When we don't ask those crucial questions that we need to ask ourselves before we jump into some important decisions of our lives, we pay dearly for it.

Some people even take things further. They know they are doing something wrong but still choose to keep doing it, either because they can't help themselves or simply don't care. That was the case with the prodigal son. The best way he probably thought he could achieve freedom was to ask for his own portion of his father's wealth, then run as far away as he could from his country, far beyond the watchful eyes of everyone, and there indulge in any lifestyle he chooses. However, he was wrong. Life taught him a bitter lesson.

Habits

Repeated behaviors lead to habits. Habits announce or give us up anywhere we go. We take them with us. We use them to make the world heaven or hell. We use them to make our lives better or bitter. The prodigal son did not develop the habit of a wild lifestyle overnight. He must have nursed and experimented with it for a while at home and in his city of abode. The more he fed his appetite, the more the appetite asked for more until things got out of hand, and his life spiraled into the decision to escape to a place where he will have no boundaries. I am sure he loved his father, his sibling, and everyone in his father's household, but that couldn't stop him from leaving. I am sure he loved being a part of the family business, but that couldn't stop him. Even the beauty of his city, the familiar sights, and the sounds of his neighborhood couldn't stop him because he had become a slave to his desires.

Proverbs 14:12 says,

"There is a way that seems right to a man, but its end is the way of death..."

When our desires drive us, nothing matters anymore. All we want to do is to pursue whatever seems right to us without thinking about the consequences.

Making excuses

How many times have you looked for a reason to escape to a place where you will have the opportunity to do and act as you like? Some lie to their spouses regularly. They cook up stories of non-existing workloads as their reasons for staying longer than usual in the office. But the real reason is they just want to feed their carnal appetites with one sin or the other after their normal work hours. Some would plan a job trip to another city or country just to have the opportunity to stay away from home and from the watchful eyes of family members as they live their riotous life, just like the prodigal son. Some are so thrilled to escape from home every time their job creates the opportunity for them to travel or stay longer at work, not because they love their job so much, but because it allows them to feed their ungodly appetites.

Some are fortunate to make it back from such journeys without much collateral damage to their health or family, but some don't. Some bring back venereal diseases or demonic spirits that may end up tormenting them all their lives. Some may find a new lifestyle they never had, and before they know it, they become hooked.

Are you happy each time you have the opportunity to leave your family for a while? If so, why? At one time, maybe the prodigal son may have felt it was becoming more problematic to escape the watchful eyes of his elder brother or his father or his father's hired servants. He may have felt the town or city they lived in had little or no fun. Whatever got into him made him a slave or servant of his desires. He was helpless. He wanted to escape, and escape he did. He escaped to a far-away country, dragged by his insatiable desires for a wild lifestyle.

What are those things in your life that have imprisoned you? What are the choices you make daily that serve as triggers to your bad habits? Maybe, it's time to stop feeding the habit and start starving it. Maybe, it's time to come to your senses and ask yourself some tough questions. Maybe, it's time to go through the school of self-examination, which may help you put the necessary breaks in your life. Your choices have consequences. They make or break you. Maybe you have lost your marriage because of your past choices; maybe you have lost your house or car because of your past choices; maybe you have lost your freedom. So did the prodigal son, but one day he stopped making excuses for his habits; one day, he came to his senses and decided to begin again, which made all the difference.

The veil of blindness

The Bible declares:

"³But even if our gospel is veiled, it is veiled to those who are perishing, ⁴whose minds the god of this age has blinded, who do not believe, lest the light of the gospel of the glory of Christ, who is the image of God, should shine on them" **2 Corinthians 4:3-4.**

The scripture above makes an important point. It points to the fact that the god of this world plays a role in the lives of unbelievers. He plays the game of deception. The devil knows how to decorate sin to make it look appetizing while making people blind to the poison or bait hidden inside it. The reason some people live the type of life they live is that they are walking in darkness. There are veils over their eyes that make them not see beyond their desires. It's this spiritual blindness that pushes some people to indulge in all sorts of depraved and riotous living like the prodigal son. It's the blindness that leads the pleasure hunter to grab whatever that pleases his eyes or gives him temporary gratification. It's the blindness that causes many to experiment with deadly and addictive things.

It's the same blindness that made the prodigal son make the foolish decision to ask for his inheritance at a young age. Thank God he came back to his senses after scales of worldliness were knocked off his eyes by the hands of adversity. It was after the blinders fell off that he began to see his mistakes. When he began to re-evaluate his lifestyle, he began to see that there was more to life than met the eye.

One of the worst characteristics of the fallen nature of man is blindness. But no matter the level of your blindness, it is not a permanent scar or defect unless you make it one. The prodigal son made many bad choices by plunging himself into the wild lifestyle of a strange and far away land, squandering every penny he had after a short while, and getting caught up in a bad case of famine; still, his story had a happy ending. The difference between him and some people who are still trapped is that he came to his senses and made the sensible choice to turn his back to his old lifestyle and head back to his family's security.

To reason or not to reason

Isaiah 1:18 says, **"'Come now, and let us reason together,' Says the LORD..."**

Some Christians believe that there is no place for the use of reasoning in Christianity. They are so spiritually minded that they stop engaging in the use of their common sense in solving problems. A lot of problems can be solved with proper reasoning with the brain God gave you. Sometimes I feel we bother God too much with every irrelevant thing. Apart from reasoning with God through quality prayer and fellowship time, reasoning with God also means using your brain to make daily right choices that the Spirit of God gives you the green light.

Some people go as far as refusing doctors' help when they are

sick, forgetting that the physician is not the healer. He is only
a vessel in the hands of God. Many people go to an early grave
because they refused to apply the wisdom of reasoning. In
colleges, there have been stories of Christians who refused to
study for their tests because of the wrong belief system. They
believe that they can substitute the time for their studies with
the time for evangelism and still do exceptionally well in their
exams. Some of them end up failing woefully in their school
tests.

The Bible emphasizes the truth that,

"¹To everything *there is* a season,
A time for every purpose under heaven:
²A time to be born,
And a time to die;
A time to plant,
And a time to pluck *what is* planted;
³A time to kill,
And a time to heal;
A time to break down,
And a time to build up;
⁴A time to weep,
And a time to laugh;
A time to mourn,
And a time to dance;
⁵A time to cast away stones,
And a time to gather stones;
A time to embrace,
And a time to refrain from embracing;
⁶A time to gain,
And a time to lose;

A time to keep,
And a time to throw away;
⁷A time to tear,
And a time to sew;
A time to keep silent,
And a time to speak;
⁸A time to love,
And a time to hate;
A time of war,
And a time of peace."

Ecclesiastes 3:1-8

Indeed, there is time to reason. When the prodigal son engaged his reasoning in re-evaluating his lifestyle, he turned a new leaf. Coming to his senses may have involved seeking to know God's purpose in his life or facing the realities of the damages he has done to his life: the pain he has caused his parents and other troubling things he has done. No one preached the gospel of repentance to him. He talked to himself for a long time until he snapped out of his foolishness until he realized it was time to begin the journey back to his father. If we take time to examine ourselves and our actions, it may point us to the path back to our heavenly father. The prodigal son's choices to re-evaluate his life helped him find the courage and strength to begin the journey home, and in the end, rewriting the story of his life.

Small beginnings

Do not despise or underestimate small beginnings because Job 1:21 says, **"Though your beginning was small, yet your** latter end would increase abundantly."

Though the steps the prodigal son took when he came to his senses seemed like little initial steps, but they were significant. When you begin a journey, every step you take in the right direction will bring you closer to your destination. Recognize little improvements in your life and in the lives of others. Appreciate your children or spouse, or friend when they make little progress in their battles; that may encourage them to do more.

Zechariah 4:10 says,

"For who has despised the day of small things?
For these seven rejoice to see
The plumb line in the hand of Zerubbabel.
They are the eyes of the LORD,
Which scan to and fro throughout the whole earth."

If you are going through a battle, do not quit because you made only a little progress. If you keep trusting God and saturating your life with His infallible Word, the Bible, sooner than you think, you will win your battle. Your job is to keep taking the steps towards freedom, no matter how small they are, and the mighty hands of God will propel you to the finish line. He has rebuilt and rescued many lives, and He will do it for you.

The place of grace

Sometimes it's good to remember that grace plays an important factor in each of our lives. Romans 9:16 says, **"So then *it is* not of him who wills, nor of him who runs, but of God who shows mercy."**

This verse of scripture is the classical definition of grace; the unadulterated, unmitigated, unquantifiable and unmerited favor of God. In the words of the late 19th century/early 20th-century eminent theologian Benjamin B. Warfield,

"Grace is free sovereign favor to the ill-deserving."

Don't be quick to write yourself or other people off. You may not see what God sees in your life or in the lives of others. Don't push people out of the door when God has not finished shaping and prefabricating them. With your mortal eyes, you may not immediately see what God is seeing in them. Or you may not know what God wants to do with their lives. If you encourage anyone who makes a little right choice in fixing his life, he may take another step towards redemption. But if you put him down, he may lose the courage to continue. If you add your strength to the little strength he has, the obstacle may become easier to overcome. If you add your faith to his little faith, both of you could end up climbing the mountain he has struggled for years to climb.

Freedom is a precious thing to everyone. It's worth making a little sacrifice to help someone find or experience it. Don't spend too much time on endless theological arguments. Instead, take that time to be the vessel through which the grace of God can flow into the lives of those fighting a battle or the other; or those dealing with the consequences of their bad choices. If, by the grace of God, they turn a new leaf, you would not have lived in vain. Sometimes, what matters is not the size of your church or your Bible but the lives you touched through the investments you made in them, even when it was not convenient.

Food for thought

- Better decisions are made when you are true to yourself and to others around you. You can't have freedom when you constantly infringe on the freedom of others.

- Those that live in denial will always avoid those who point them to the truth. If you avoid light, you will always wallow in darkness.

- Hard choices are the hallmarks of those who value freedom. If you love your freedom, you will not fall into the little temptations that many fall to every day. Without freedom as armor, you will be vulnerable to any little attack or temptation.

- Those things you embrace in a hurry leave the biggest scars on you because they pierce deeper.

- A friend is only a friend if he or she helps you make the right choices and decisions. You don't need a friend who makes no positive contribution to your life.

- You may never recover in a lifetime what you lose or surrender in a single wrong choice or decision.

- Before you make a decision, put a price tag on it. Most times, the immediate reward of making one wrong decision is not worth the long-term penalty you will have to pay for it.

- Without holding unto the guardrails of freedom, you will be flung in every direction in the roller-coaster of life until you are thrown off the cliff.

CHAPTER FOUR

THE SECOND LAW OF FREEDOM

The second law of freedom: *Freedom is not sustainable without a lifestyle of self-examination.*

The story of the prodigal son gives us a lot of meat to chew. What made him abandon his home for a far-away country? Yes, as earlier stated, he probably wanted to escape from the watchful eyes of all the members of his family to have the freedom to live whatever lifestyle he desired. He did not know that true freedom is not having the right or liberty to do whatever you want but having the will and power to do what is right.

The prodigal son probably knew his father was very kind and would succumb to his request for his own inheritance, so he took advantage of it. This is typical of many of us. We like to take advantage of people or situations at any given opportunity, not minding if it is the right thing to do. Some husbands like to take advantage of their wives' kindness, some wives like to take advantage of their husbands' laissez-faire attitude, and some children like to take advantage of their rich and old parents. Most times, we are focused on the immediate gain or the short-term gratification than the long-term effect. But years later, many people live with the guilt of such bad decisions. The prodigal son was one of such people. After swimming in the ocean of his runaway desires for some time, then he came to the same conclusion that Solomon came to when he said,

"I have seen all the works that are done under the sun; and indeed, all is vanity and grasping for the wind" (Ecclesiastes 1:14).

Adversities

One of the most exciting moments in life is those times you have a lot of money in your hands to spend. You feel important when you walk into a store, and if you are a teenager, you are less likely going to be very particular about the price tags of items you want. Whether you are buying a gold ring or a new car, or custom furniture, when you have a lot of money in your hand to spend, you will find yourself singing and dancing to any music that filters into your ears on your way to the store. Sometimes, it is that excitement that causes you to overspend. That may have been the case with the prodigal son. When he arrived in the far away city with a lot of money and was suddenly surrounded by the bells and whistles of opulent stores and restaurants, he was probably caught in the excitement of a new life in a new place that he might have over extended himself financially within the first few weeks of arrival.

Everyone knows that a huge bank account can evaporate within minutes with a visit to places like 5th Avenue in New York, Causeway Bay in Hong Kong, Avenue des Champs-

Elysees in Paris, New Bond Street in London, or Via Monte Napoleone in Milan. The prodigal son probably settled in one of those exclusive neighborhoods. If he did, he lived above his means, and that was not without grave consequences. It may have triggered the successive events that eventually threw him into untold hardship and adversities.

The Bible says,

"¹⁴But when he had spent all, there arose a severe famine in that land, and he began to be in want. ¹⁵Then he went and joined himself to a citizen of that country, and he sent him into his fields to feed swine. ¹⁶And he would gladly have filled his stomach with the [a]pods that the swine ate, and no one gave him *anything*."

Luke 15: 14-16

Nothing rewrites the stories of our lives faster than adverse circumstances. It took an avalanche of adversities to knock the prodigal son back to his senses (Luke 15:17). They made him ask himself some hard questions. They made him switch from the high gears of the fast lane lifestyle to the slow gears of self-examination. And that yielded great results.

Who could have believed that this flamboyant and ubiquitous young man with a lot of money to spend would be thrust into diverse adversities in his dream land? Who would have believed that he would be so famished that he would long for pigs' leftover meals? What does it take for someone to be so hungry that he is willing to eat anything? For years while the prodigal son lived with his father, he had much to eat, so he never had the slightest taste of the cruel pangs of hunger until he left home and fell into adversities.

Being caught up in the Nigeria–Biafra war at a young age, I tasted hunger. My dad was studying in London when the war started. Things got very bad for us without a father at home to help. Many times, we had little or nothing to eat. I was only ten years old and couldn't help Mom to provide for my siblings and me. It was a horrendous time, to say the least. Millions of Biafrans died from the pains of hunger and the torments of malnutrition. Corpses were a common sight as people died daily in droves. There was no scarcity of people looking like skeletons left only with bloated stomachs and prominent rib cages because of the toll of Kwashiorkor. It's no exaggeration to say that hunger is a vulture that eats human flesh with joy.

I would imagine that the prodigal son came close to my war experience with hunger. It took the harrowing pains of hunger, the laborious and dirty job of feeding pigs, and the harsh realities of dwelling in dry and barren land for him to come to his senses. Even the deaf listens when adversity speaks.

Introspection

This attainment in sensibility did not materialize without a sustained period of introspection. Freedom is hardly attainable and sustainable without a lifestyle of self-examination. The period of self-examination is the time you become honest with yourself. It's the time you mull over your past choices and the unnecessary prices you have paid for some of them. It's a time with reality and the truth you must confront.

A crucial time came when the prodigal son asked himself the honest question. "What am I doing starving to death in a strange and far away land while my father's servants have more than enough to eat?" (Luke 15:17). Maybe, he asked the subsequent question, "What if I die in this land with none of my parents or my brother here to say goodbye?" Or maybe, that was the time he asked the rhetorical question, "Is it not better to be a beggar in my father's house than to be working in a pig farm?" After this period of self-examination, he came to his senses. He decided it was time to abandon his foolishness, swallow his pride, and say goodbye to the far away country stinking with poverty. He packed his bags and headed home.

Too often, we forget that wherever we go, freedom has its boundaries or laws guiding it. And whether they are divine laws of God or man-made laws, breaking them have their repercussions. What did it cost the prodigal son when he broke some of the laws of freedom? Oh, it reduced him to a beggar; it stripped him every bit of his dignity. It made him to know the real taste of hunger, the type that pushes people to the garbage bin, even if the bin belonged to a bunch of dirty pigs. His initial reckless disregard for some of the cardinal laws of freedom led to his downfall.

What price have you paid for breaking the laws of freedom? Maybe you have been very fortunate so far. You have not paid much price, but I guarantee you that if you continue to break these laws, there will come a payday. Maybe, you have hidden that bad habit or lifestyle from the eyes of men. You may have fooled your spouse for years that now you think you are very smart, too smart to be caught. I have news for you. There is always a payday. But if you come to your senses today and begin to retrace your steps as the prodigal son did, your story may end well. After the period of remorse and emergence from the crucibles of self-examination, he found the courage to begin the journey that ended with a father's embrace and forgiveness.

Self-examination is a forgotten virtue, a road seldom traveled by many. In my quest to be free and to stay free, I found out that it has great redemptive powers. You can fight and defeat the enemy, you know, but that's not the case with the enemy lurking in the dark, unknown to you. Self-examination helps you discover your enemy's identity and tricks, giving you a greater opportunity to defeat your enemy or escape his ambush.

Hosea 4:6 says,

"My people are destroyed for lack of knowledge.
Because you have rejected knowledge,
I also will reject you from being priest for Me;
Because you have forgotten the law of your God,
I also will forget your children."

Self-examination empowers you with tremendous knowledge and foresight needed to confront everyday travails of life, especially for the Christian who wants to put on the whole armor for warfare. It's one of the most valuable navigating instruments that can lead you to the road to discovery and recovery. It's one of the most important first steps to take in the walk to freedom. It has a way of creating enough passage for you to pass through in times of adversity. If you make it your daily friend, your life will not remain the same.

Sustaining your freedom

If you ask rich people the greatest challenge with being rich, most of them would say it's the fear of losing their wealth. It's as hard remaining rich as it is acquiring the wealth. It's as hard staying on top as it is hard getting to the top. Now you get it! It's as hard remaining free as it is becoming free. So, what do you do to keep your freedom? What did the prodigal son do to sustain his freedom?

- **Evaluation**

After spending the time re-evaluating his life and doing all the reality checks he could, he owned up his mistakes. But he didn't stop there. Many things could sabotage his decision to return home. How does he escape from the clutches of the city and the city life? He may have sat down one night and drawn up a plan. So, he needed to know what to tell his old party friends or partners in crime; how to prepare for the long journey back home with no penny in his pocket, and how to extricate himself, without a hitch, from the pit he threw himself into. He probably didn't want anybody to know his plan to return home, especially those capable of luring him back to his old life. He probably was hiding and tiptoeing around in the last few days before his departure to make sure his plans succeeded. However, despite all the planning, what probably helped him the most was the long hours of evaluation and re-evaluation of his life.

- **Stay home**

After he got home, he never left or ran away again! He submitted himself willingly to the watchful eyes of his father, his brother and others living with them. That is to say; it's not enough to come to your senses; there is more to saying I am sorry; there is more to confessing your sins and returning to God. If you don't stay home, or in the church, or in the environment that will hold you accountable, your victory may be short-lived.

In John 8:11, Jesus turned to the woman caught in adultery and said,

"...go and sin no more."

For this woman caught in adultery to abide by this instruction, she must run far away from her customers. If she does not remove herself from her old environment and surround herself with the right people, she may slip back into her old life. The decision to come home is as important as the decision to surround yourself with people who will make you stronger and better, people you can draw strength from: not people who will quickly put out your precious little light.

The prodigal son went home and submitted himself to the watchful eyes of a loving father, and that made a whole world of difference. If you are fighting a battle, stay with those whose swords are sharp enough to rip off your chains of slavery and not those who are in the same shoes with you. That is one way to sustain your freedom. That was what the prodigal son did. You can do the same today by returning to the arms of your heavenly Father and refusing to leave his presence again.

- **Getting back to work**

Another important way to sustain your freedom is to get back to work. When the prodigal son returned home, he went back to the family business. When you return to God, get your hands busy. When you return home to your family, go back to work. When you return to your church, find something to do, especially something you love. If you love to sing, join the choir. If you love to smile, join the ushering team. If you stay busy in the right job and with the right people, you are more likely to retain your freedom and salvation.

One of the greatest ministries often neglected, especially in Africa, is rehabilitation. There are very few rehabilitation centers in Africa. With proper help and care, people can recover from different addictions or be completely delivered from lifestyles they have battled with for years. In Africa, we pray for them and then abandon them. That's why we have very little result with people caught in the crossfire with the teething problem of addiction. Sometimes we use prayer as a means of running away from the tedious process of rehabilitation. Ministry does not involve only praying and preaching to people; it also involves feeding the hungry, clothing the naked and rehabilitating the addict.

Some people may not have a good home like the prodigal son. The father was wealthy and had so much love for his son. He probably made sure that he never removed his eyes away from his son after he returned home. He probably prayed more for him, cared more for him, and went any extra needed mile to provide for him anything that would help his complete rehabilitation and reintegration. He probably avoided reminding him he was a failure at any little provocation. He probably started him with a lighter workload to give him time to heal. It takes a lot of wisdom and patience to deal with people who had been through failures and are trying to put all that behind them. It takes a lot of brokenness and sacrifices. It takes a lot of dedication and love; the type God has for us.

Lamentations 3:22 says,

"*Through* the LORD's mercies, we are not consumed,

Because His compassions fail not."

Don't bring back your gods

Another way to sustain your freedom is never to bring back your gods from Babylon or Egypt. Everywhere you visit, if you look closely at the people, you will find the god they serve. Some serve the god of fashion, some the god of mammon, some the god of immorality. If you value your Christian faith and your relationship with the only true God, don't take your god (idol) with you when you leave your land of captivity.

The prodigal son departed without the gods of the far away land. He probably gathered all the idols he accumulated and set them on fire shortly after he returned to his senses. He abandoned the old lifestyle. He came back home with a repentant heart. If the prodigal son had brought his idols home, he would inevitably return to worshipping them. When you return to God, build a new altar for God, for He is the only true God. Every other foundation is faulty; every other god is a false god.

Food for thoughts

- You can walk away from freedom on your own accord, but that is not the case when you are in captivity. It's easy to surrender your freedom, but it's not easy for your captive chains to surrender you.

- When you walk into any bondage, it takes ownership of your life, but when you walk daily in the corridors of freedom, you take ownership of your life and destiny.

- The day you begin to look before you walk or jump is the day you begin to chart the course of success and to build a strong hedge of protection around yourself.

- Until you give up the habit of making excuses, freedom will remain a farfetched dream. People who constantly make excuses are marked and marred by self-inflicted injuries.

- Whatever you are afraid of will always defeat or imprison you. Don't live a day fearing what you have an inherent power to defeat. Fear is nothing but accepting defeat before engaging in a fight.

- One day of self-examination is worth more than one year of living an unexamined life.

CHAPTER FIVE

THE THIRD LAW OF FREEDOM

The third law of freedom: *Do not ignore any symptom, no matter how little it is.*

One of the saddest things that can happen to a man is to go for his annual medical checkup and to be told a few days later that he has terminal cancer. The disease has invaded his body for some time and has done a lot of damage unnoticed. Looking back now, he probably remembers a few minor symptoms that cropped up months ago that he quickly dismissed as nothing.

It's easy to ignore little symptoms. We assume they are nothing to worry about, but sometimes such assumptions can be dangerous and costly. As finite beings, we don't know; there is a lot we don't see. That's why over the years, scientists have invented different tools and apparatuses to help us physically see more of the invisible microbial and cellular world.

The hideous nature of some diseases underscores the fact that annual medical examination is essential to a healthy lifestyle and longevity. Unfortunately, many cannot afford a yearly medical checkup because they don't have medical insurance or the money to foot the medical bills. Sadly, many of them end up paying dearly for it, sometimes with their lives.

No matter how little, symptoms are necessary alarms that crop up to help warn us about the advent of insidious diseases. No matter how small, never ignore any symptom. This is one major thing keeping the average lifespan of Africans lower than usual.

The good news is that there is a type of checkup everyone can afford. This type of checkup does not require the trained eyes and sophisticated instruments of a physician, nor does it place any financial burden on anyone. All that is required is a few minutes of your time each day. This free and easy check-up is called self-examination. It's a good prophylactic measure both for physical and non-physical symptoms.

Sin starts with a small grip on someone. That was probably the problem the young prodigal son had. He probably ignored the longer than usual stares at neighborhood girls, which indicates a little weed of lust growing inside his heart! Perhaps, he did not pay attention to the extra attention he paid to the sound of nightlife. Before he knew it, these little symptoms grew into desires he could not control. The more they grew, the more his impatience and greed also grew until things spiraled out of control, leading to his leaving home to a place where he could freely feed his appetites. The heart is an open field; if you don't weed it constantly, it will be overrun by weeds. The prodigal son knew that in order to sustain the wild desires that have taken him captive, he needed a lot of money. His father was rich, so he knew he would get a lot of money from him if he requested his inheritance. As soon as he got the money, he left home.

Don't get caught unawares

To avoid the mistakes the prodigal son made, you must not allow yourself to be caught unawares. The world is swamped with godless fads and doctrines of materialism, so a structured life of self-examination can be a very good weapon of offense and defense for those serious about leading a life of freedom and dignity. Great leaders, and even ordinary people with the desire to finish strong in life, always create the time to stop in front of the mirror to take a deep look at their hearts. They do not leave their lives to chance. They employ the strong hands of self-examination to put the needed breaks in their lives as they navigate the dangerous terrains of life. In the end, they save themselves from the countless hardships and pain which the prodigal son put himself through.

It's easy to ignore little blemishes in your character or morals. You may even assume you are not as bad as your neighbor. For this reason, many have failed to deal with the little foxes in their lives, making a shipwreck of their marriages, careers, or their Christian faith. Many have fallen from their thrones and lost their crowns because they ignored a little smothering fire, and before they knew it, they were engulfed by its flames.

One of America's most important founding fathers whose head is on the $100 bill, Benjamin Franklin, said,

"An ounce of prevention is worth a pound of cure."

If you leave a few little weeds unattended, they will become a forest in a few months. Galatians 5:9 tells us that **"A little leaven leavens the whole lump."**

For emphasis, may I remind you that we live in a world full of traps and webs of deceptions, a world constantly dangling all kinds of destructive wares before our eyes everywhere we turn? This world is full of distractions and untold evil schemes. Therefore, it will be unwise to live an unguarded life or a life devoid of constant self-examination. As it's dangerous to travel an unknown path at night, so it is for the man that is undertaking the journey of life without the floodlight of self-examination.

Guard your heart

The heart should be guarded jealously. It should be guarded every minute of every day because of the significant role it plays in our everyday life.

Proverb 4:23 says,

**"Keep your heart with all diligence,
For out of it *spring* the issues of life."**

This scripture highlights the importance of the heart and the reason it must be guarded. Everywhere you go, there are different types of dross spreading like plagues; dross that can easily envelop an unguarded heart.

Be careful with the type of books you read. Be careful with the type of music you listen to. Be careful with the type of men's philosophies and doctrines you expose yourself to. Be careful with the type of people you hang around.

Recently, I heard a story that shocked me, an ordeal a Christian family went through not too long ago with their first son. After their son graduated from a renowned University in America, he got a very good job. They were very proud of him and were grateful to God for blessing him with a very well-paying job. Weeks later, their son relocated from the city they lived in another city to start the job.

Shortly after starting the job, he met a young, charismatic Muslim man in the firm he was working, and they became friends. A year later in his new job, he called his parents and told them that he has converted to Islam. They were devastated. In their wildest dream, they never expected such news. What is remarkable about this story is that this young man who suddenly fell for Islam was raised in a Pentecostal church. Both of his parents are seasoned born-again Christians who, over the years, taught all their children the tenets of the Christian faith and the precepts of faithfully following and serving Christ. So how and why did their son stray away from the truth? Maybe he had started backsliding before he left home. Perhaps he spent too much time with his friend and was exposed to too many sugar-coated lies. The devil is very crafty. We have to be watchful at all time.

Choose your friends and church carefully. There are too many spiritual poisons out there. There are too many wolves in sheep's clothing.

1 John 4:1 says,

"Beloved, do not believe every spirit, but test the spirits to see whether they are from God because many false prophets have gone out into the world."

The danger with heart pollution is that it's subtle. Too many times, too many people's hearts are poisoned and polluted before they realize it. Sometimes, it's hard for them to recover from the damage done to their hearts or the poison they have already consumed.

When a man's heart is covered with dross, his beauty quickly fades away. He becomes a changed person and might even become a burden to himself and society. Sometimes, people infected with a contagious disease may not know they are carrying and infecting other people with a dangerous contagion.

The principal thing in the heart of God is to see us conform to the image of His dear son, Jesus Christ. His heart's desire is to mold and shapes us into firebrands, people he can use to set the world ablaze with the light of the Gospel of redemption. But when your life is covered with dross, you become buried in the pit of self-delusion or by the whims and caprices of your desires.

Proverbs 25:4 warns us to,

**"Take away the dross from silver,
And it will go to the silversmith *for* jewelry."**

Thank God there is a balm in Gilead to make the wounded whole again (Jeremiah 8:22). Through the power of the redemptive blood of Jesus, your dross can be washed away, and you can become a liberated soul.

When the chains are broken, and your heart is cleansed by the blood of Jesus Christ, your beauty will be seen; you will become a city set on a hill that cannot be hidden (Matthew 5:14-16).

Your light will glow brighter than the stars of heaven. You will become a jewel to your family, friends, society, and, more importantly, to God.

Food for thoughts

- Freedom begins by imprisoning things that want to imprison you. Don't feed your fears; don't feed your unhealthy habits. Starve them to death.

- Don't treat the ailment of any form of bondage with half the required pill or with the wrong medication. It will only worsen your case.

- Whatever you associate with will somehow leave its marks on you. You can't keep going to the place that feeds your lust or bad habit without being hooked or enslaved. If you don't want to get wet, stay out of the rain or shower; if you don't want to soil your hands, don't touch any vile or dirty thing with your hands.

- Some have fallen from their throne because they ignored the little foxes. Others have lost their crowns because they ignored little smothering fires, and before they knew it, they were engulfed by their flames.

- The heart is an open field; if you don't weed it constantly, it would be overrun by weeds.

Ikechi Akurunwa

CHAPTER SIX

THE FOURTH LAW OF FREEDOM

The fourth law of freedom: ***Don't remain on the ground; you don't belong there!***

The ground is a place of captivity. This is why when any man succumbs to death; he is laid down in the belly of the ground. While you are still alive, you don't belong there. You are too precious to be chained to its prison walls with its hard, coarse and callous hands. When you trip and fall, get up. The ground has no poultice or tender arms to soothe your pains.

The ground could be the low places of life we find ourselves sometimes. It could be a failed marriage, the loss of a spouse or child; the dark pit of poverty; the bondage of addiction, or other things that have imprisoned us. Sometimes, the pain could be overpowering; still, the ground has nothing to do for you other than to create more pain.

When you are on the ground, your feeling will be one of your greatest enemies. It plays a significant role in how long you will strap yourself to the ground. There is also the fear of getting up and falling again. I have been there. It can be very real. At every glance at the circumstances surrounding you, all you hear is the drumbeat of fear and doubt. This is the reason people drop out of college, or quit trying to fix their marriages, or quit looking for a job, or stop taking their medications and fighting for a cause.

There was a time in my life I was sick and thought I wouldn't make it. At that point, I looked forward to death instead of to healing. I was in my twenties then; now, I am in my early sixties. My life turned around when I started rejecting death and believing in God for healing and longevity. You are better than what you think you are, stronger than you know, and of much value than you think you are. If you get knocked down, get up. Allow yourself to fight again, and maybe, rewrite your story.

When you are on the ground, people will step on you or use you as a stepping stone. When you are on the ground, you will hear the loud echoes of failure and the whispers of naysayers more than ever before. The ground is a cursed place.

Genesis 3:17 says,

"Cursed *is* the ground for your sake;
In toil you shall eat *of* it
All the days of your life."

No matter your theology on why God cursed the ground instead of Adam, the ground still remains a place of

disadvantage. Don't remain on the ground. No winner does. The prodigal son didn't remain in the land that stripped him of his pride and dignity. He didn't remain in the land where he almost starved to death. One day he got up from the ashes of defeat, dusted himself and headed home. He said:
**"I will arise and go to my father, and will say to him, "Father, I have sinned against heaven and before you..."
(Luke 15:18).**

There are times when you fall to the ground and sustain serious injuries, and you can't get up on your own. That is a hard place to be, but it's at such times that you will know those who really care about you or those who are your true friends. Maybe you lost your house and can't find someone to open his or her door to you. You may be so sick that you need someone to help lift you up from the bed to go to the bathroom, and there is hardly anyone around to treat you with love and respect and alleviate your pains and suffering. As hard as those times can be, you cannot give up. Sometimes you have to fight for your life with all the strength you have. That's what the prodigal son did. At the lowest point in his life, he decided to rise from the ground. He began by deciding to give himself a second chance. That singular decision led him to muster enough strength to plan and execute his trip back home.

The good news is that there are still good people out there. If you decide to get up from the ground, you will be surprised by the number of people eager to help you stand to your feet. The battles of life are not fought alone. If you are patient enough, you will find people ready to build a bridge across the valley you have waited years to cross. When the prodigal son fell on the ground of poverty, humiliation and hopelessness, possibly his friends ran away. Still, his father was in front of his house every day, waiting for him to return. His father was ready to bestow back to him all he had lost. Yes, his father was his lifeline, but he was miles away from his father. Without the determination to live, without a resolute decision to surmount every challenge surrounding him, he wouldn't have made it back to the waiting arms of his father.

We must fight and push through the rubbles of our life until we find our lifeline. There is always someone out there who is our destiny helper, but too many times, we don't have the patience and the endurance to take the extra needed step to get to our destiny helpers. If the prodigal son had given up his plan to go home because of his overwhelming circumstances, he would have remained in his misery, and probably he would have died a lonely and sorrowful death. But he knew better. He knew if he found a way to get back to his father, he could be given a second chance.

For you, the helper may not be your father; it may be a stranger. The world is full of undiscovered angels willing to help those who muster up enough courage to rise from the ground to seek help.

In one of my poems, I wrote:

When birds sing their melodious songs
and flowers spread their auburn wings
and smile to those who stare;

when the sun stretches its hands
to cloth the earth with warmth
and the sweet smell of lavender
makes the air soothing and refreshing;

when snow clothes the mountain
with its elegant white robe
and rain moistens parched lands
to give life to moribund seeds;

when the sky adorns itself with hues of gold
and sometimes builds white thrones
and blue castles to thrill
the eyes of nature lovers;

when the moon sheds its luminous
light on dark lonely paths
and stars dance and glow at twilight
to cheer pilgrims at crossroads;

they all are affirming that everyone
has something to give to make
the world a better place.

And all you have to do each day
is to strive to make your own little difference,
and to be gracious to the love of others.

Indeed, the prodigal son was gracious to his father's love. When he got home, his father threw a party for him and adorned him with a costly robe and ring.

You may not have a rich father or brother who could restore your former glory but, don't despair. God specializes in stepping in when we turn our attention from man to Him. Have you read, **"It is better to trust in the LORD than to put confidence in man?"** (Psalm 118:8). And on the same note, Jeremiah 17:5 warns,

"Cursed *is* the man who trusts in man
And makes flesh his strength,
Whose heart departs from the LORD."

A lot of African rural community pastors are still going through financial hell. The case of a pastor who hails from my town easily comes to mind. This pastor is one of the men of God whose lives had a significant impact on me. For over fifteen years, he pastored churches in villages. One day, about a week before I left Nigeria to attend a conference in the U.S, he broke the very sad news to me. We met at one of our most popular village market squares. He was with his wife. After the initial pleasantries, a sudden gloom descended over his face. Then he looked into my eyes and dropped the bombshell. "Mac, I am leaving the ministry."

I was shocked. I was at a loss for words as I stared at him in unbelief. "I am going to the city of Abuja to look for something else to do," he blurted out. Then after a short pause, he went on to tell me a little of what he had been through over the years as a rural community pastor. I was utterly speechless at the end of his story. He left me sad and saddled with many questions. They were so poor that many times they had no food to eat. He turned his back at one point in his story and showed me the torn pant he was wearing. To him, nobody cared about his welfare or that of his family. As far as he was concerned, he had had it. He was not going to put his family through hardship anymore.

As I learnt years later, this pastor, after quitting the ministry and headed to Abuja, he lost his peace. There was a battle inside his soul for quitting the ministry. He fought as hard as he could to no avail. So, after living through the torment of rebellion against his assignment, he went back to being a pastor. The problem was he trusted in the arm of flesh for his sustenance. Thank God he came back to his senses, like the prodigal son. Don't trust the arm of the flesh. Put your trust in the God that called you.

David knew better. In Psalms 20:7, he said, **"Some *trust* in chariots, and some in horses; But we will remember the name of the LORD our God."**

Living to fight again

If you keep your head above the water, you will likely not drown. If you keep your head up above your circumstances and don't quit, you will live to fight again. In one of my poems titled *The discounted man,* I wrote:

The dried well of his soul
has gathered water again
after many years of desolation.

Who would have thought
that after those long years
of misery and shame,
after those countless hours

of laying like a pile of ashes,
and wallowing daily
in the mire of grief and self-pity,
all those who gave up on him
would one day
drink from his well again?

Oh, never discount a man
whose heart is still beating.
Never say to him,
you will never rise again,
you will never sing again,
you will never dance again,
you will never dream again.

When the sudden awakening
that descends after experiencing
failure came upon him,
he rose with vim and vigor
and shoveled out layers upon layers
of decay, dirt, and death from his well,
day after day,
till water began to rise.

And now, from the depth
of his rejuvenated soul,
the waters of grace and candor
are offered to everyone who comes
to drink of the wisdom of someone
who has seen both sides of life.

Oh, never discount a man
whose heart is still beating.
Never say to him,
you will never rise again,
you will never sing again,
you will never dance again,
you will never dream again.

The decision to regain your freedom lies in your hand. The journey to freedom begins when you decide to rise from the ground and take the first step of faith down the road to freedom. Like the father of the prodigal son, your heavenly father is daily waiting for you to rise up from the ground of defeat and discouragement and reach for His outreached arm. Never discount yourself or a man whose heart is still beating; never say to yourself, "I don't think I can make it." Or say to a man whose heart is still beating, "You will never rise again, you will never sing again, you will never dance again, or you will never dream again. Never say "Never!"

Food for thought

- If you are climbing the hill of freedom and you keep looking down in fear, you will likely not make it to the top.

- If you paddle the boat of freedom with the wrong paddle, you will be swallowed by the waves in the middle of the sea of life.

- It doesn't matter how many times you have been told that you are a failure; what matters is how many times you have told yourself that you are a winner and truly believe that you are, indeed, a winner.

- No one can defeat an enemy with both of his hands shackled. You are as strong as you are free.

- It's harder to get up from the ground with your hands and feet in cuffs than when your hands and feet are free. If you want to go far in life, make sure unhealthy habits do not tie your hands and feet.

- If you keep your head above the water, you will likely not drown. If you keep your head up above your circumstances and don't quit, you will emerge a winner one day. Winners fight till the end or till they cross the finish line.

- Gravity always wants to pull you to the ground because it knows if it can keep you on the ground, it will be harder for you to jump over your mountains. So, the best way to beat gravity or any bondage is to grow wings. Those who constantly walk in the realms of freedom have the wings of an eagle. That's why they can daily soar over the mountains of life.

CHAPTER SEVEN

THE FIFTH LAW OF FREEDOM

The fifth law of freedom: *As long as your heart is still beating, it's never too late to act.*

Yes, it's never too late to rise from the ashes of failure and defeat. It does not matter how many people that have tried and failed; give yourself another chance. It might be that all that is needed to break through your prison wall is just one more push.

Self-pity

Self-pity is one of the worst prison walls. It triggers a flood of tears that, at best, will attract a few sympathetic gestures from a few people around. With its apathetic hands, it lifts up the bandage hiding your reeking wounds for you to smell and feel sorry for yourself. It paints a dismal image of you with its teary brush, leaving you feeling as small as a miniature object that fell into a deep pit.

Some people swing between self-pity and self-gratification.

They try to kill their pain with food. At any given opportunity, they gravitate to "the way that seems right" to them as a way of pacifying themselves. They do not know they are digging a deeper hole for themselves, a hole that may lead to a catastrophic end.

Proverbs 14:12 says, **"There is a way that seems right to a man, but its end is the way to death."**

At first, the prodigal son felt he knew what to do with his life. He had it all planned out and executed it as planned. But when his plans backfired, he realized that all those ways that seemed right to him only led him to shame, disgrace, misery, trouble and more trouble. What saved him was the realization that it's **never too late to act.** He didn't drift into self-pity to the point where he could not recover. When he returned to his senses, he realized that it was not too late to begin again; it was not too late to escape from famine, and it was not too late to abandon the company of bad friends. It can never be too late to retrace one's steps to the Father! The prodigal son was ready to face humiliation, ready to go on his knees to plead for forgiveness. Nothing was going to stop him from returning home.

Don't quit the fight

No matter your situation, do not quit! Fight back. As long as you are still breathing, it's never too late to fight until you regain your lost family; it's never too late to fight until your missing child comes home; it's never too late to fight back until you break the chains of that habit. Thank God the prodigal son took the step of faith to go back home. He met with a father's love. He met acceptance and not rejection.

Luke 15:20 says,

"And he arose and came to his father. But when he was still a great way off, his father saw him and had compassion, and ran and fell on his neck and kissed him."

Oh, what he would have lost if he had not fought the fear of rejection and humiliation! What if he had believed it was too late to act or that his case was unforgivable? What if he had given up on himself or stayed back in captivity?

No matter your situation, never give up on yourself. If the prodigal son was fixated on what his hometown peers were going to say about him when they hear of his shameful story, he would not have returned. Pride is one of the sledgehammers we use to nail ourselves to the bed of defeat and self-deception. We often find it hard to swallow our pride, even when we have no good name to protect. Some people will spend their time cooking up lies they will tell their old friends when they run into them. The problem with that is that they will eventually find out the truth about your messed-up life. People are more likely to give you a second chance when you humble yourself and admit your mistakes. If you turn a new leaf, with time, people will forget about your past.

As long as you have life in you, it's never too late to fight, to recover what you have lost. It's never too late to climb out of that pit; never too late to retrace your path, and never too late to return to the waiting arms of your heavenly father. No matter the challenge at hand, do not give up hope. A great price or crown is waiting for you if you don't quit. In one of my poems, I wrote:

So, they said it can't be done;

nobody has survived such a fall,
nobody has ever recovered from such a tragedy,
and you bought the lie!

They said you can't accomplish
anything significant in life
because you don't have the qualifications
or the pedigree for such an accomplishment,
and you bought the lie!

They said you can't scale
the mountain of mediocrity
because you have no godfather
or someone in the corridors of power
to push you to the top,
and you bought the lie!

They said you would likely be a failure
because no one from your family
has ever amounted to anything,
and you bought the lie!

Didn't they tell the fern,
"You are just a plant,
you can't grow on rocks?"
But it did.

Didn't they tell the ivy,
"You have no hands,
you can't climb walls or trees?"
But it did.

Didn't they tell the mustard seed
"You are too small to grow
into a mighty tree?"
But it did.

Didn't they tell the cactus
"No plant that grows in the desert
lives longer than a few months?"
But it did.

Yes, they have told you it can't be done,
that's but the words of a mortal man.
If you believe it can be done,
one day, you too,
will prove them wrong.

The prodigal son proved those who have given up on him wrong. He made his way home, and he received a surprisingly warm reception. His efforts paid off. His come-back efforts were all worth it. The Bible says,

"And bring the fatted calf here and kill *it*, and let us eat and be merry; for this, my son was dead and is alive again; he was lost and is found.' And they began to be merry."

Luke 15: 23-24

All he probably prayed in his heart for could have been merely a little room in his father's house. He was ready to be a servant in his father's house, but his father chose to decorate him with a robe of honor and a ring of authority. Probably, when he arrived home, his clothes were in tatters; his sandals had damaged beyond repairs and were abandoned many miles away from home. But his father covered his shame by giving him sandals to wear to protect his badly worn feet from the long journey. He didn't stop there; he threw a big party for him.

The welcome party with the best of the calf they had reminds me of an old experience of mine during my college days. My father had gotten false information that I was tied down with Christian activities on the campus and was supposedly neglecting my studies. Without validating the information with me, he threatened to stop paying my school fees if I didn't discontinue the religious activities I was supposedly engaged in. My father was a very strict man, and he never gave empty threats. After weighing my options, I decided to continue serving my God in the best way I knew then. When the next school holidays came, I was afraid of going home, so I stayed back on the campus. But when my father didn't see me after about three to four months, he rescinded his threat. And without hesitation, I visited home, and to my surprise, I was given a hero's welcome. He killed a fat rooster for me, and I was served a special meal. Everybody was happy to see me. I was happy to be home, and more importantly, I was happy that I didn't back down concerning my Christian faith. Before my father died, he knelt down beside me and accepted Christ in the living room of our village house. That day was a glorious day for me.

Finishing the race

God promises a reward of eternal life to everyone who will, against all odds, defend his or her faith. And if there is a time in the history of mankind that a generation is at the brink of abandoning the Gospel for glitz and glamor, it is now. Many are ready to trade their faith for a minute kiss from the vile lips of illicit pleasure. The virtue of sticking it till the end is fast becoming a thing of the past. At a time like this, Matthew 23:13 becomes a reassuring reminder to the weary soul that,

"... he who endures to the end shall be saved."

We have a catalogue of heroes of faith who fought a good fight and finished their races, and you can be listed among them if you choose to persevere. The Bible is replete with their names.

"And what more shall I say? For the time would fail me to tell of Gideon and Barak and Samson and Jephthah, also *of* David and Samuel and the prophets: who through faith subdued kingdoms, worked righteousness, obtained promises, stopped the mouths of lions, quenched the violence of fire, escaped the edge of the sword, out of weakness were made strong, became valiant in battle, turned to flight the armies of the aliens. Women received their dead raised to life again. Others were tortured, not accepting deliverance, that they might obtain a better resurrection" (Hebrew 11:32-35).

The baton has been passed onto us, and we cannot afford to quit or fall by the wayside. We have different batons. Some have been given the baton of prayer. When they pray, things happen. Some have been given the baton of teaching. When they teach young Christian converts, their foundations become so solid and deep that no wind of adversity would be able to uproot them or shake their Christian faith. Don't discard your baton: hold onto it until you cross the finish line!

During his journey, the prodigal son probably stopped by the wayside many times, hungry and tired. He could have stopped several times to nurse his bruises: his bleeding toes or his cracked heels or to drink water from his water jug. He probably tried flagging down some drivers for a ride but was ignored. Maybe, it was summer time, and the heat was blistering, but he never gave up. Perhaps, every step he took towards home was laborious, but he mustered all the faith he could and made it home. He stayed on course until he got home. He held onto every fiber in him until he crossed the finish line. He fought a good fight to make things right, and it can be said he finished the race as a winner.

Among all the cloud of witnesses that abound, our Savior and Master, Jesus Christ, certainly endured the most for our sakes. He never quit on you and me. Oh, how easily we quit on each other. Oh, how easily we turn our backs on each other. Oh, how easily we quit even on ourselves! Hebrews 12:2 encourages us to look unto Him so that we do not faint in our days of afflictions.

"Looking unto Jesus, the author and finisher of *our* faith, who for the joy that was set before Him endured the cross, despising the shame, and has sat down at the right hand of the throne of God."
Until you cross the finish line, don't ever quit!

Food for thoughts

- Even if everyone gives up on you, don't give up on yourself. If you hang on long enough with God, you will certainly prove to the world that you are not someone that can be easily written off.

- If you doggedly hold onto the lifeline of faith and don't give up, God will surely extend a helping hand to you. Patience has its great reward.

- He who tames his pride will be free from double standards, and there will be a refreshing fragrance of grace and candor always around him.

- There is nothing worse than pretending to be free when you are shackled from head to toe by besetting sins and habits.

- Surround yourself with people who see a way out of every problem than people who see gloom and doom in every problem.

- The voice you constantly hear or listen to every day will certainly influence your daily actions and choices.

- If you hem the edges of your life with the thread of right associations, you will build a formidable fortress around yourself at all times.

- If you cut off the loud noise of fear and doubt, there is nothing you can't accomplish in life.

- You can rewrite your story with the single habit of daily feeding your spirit with words of faith and encouragement.

- Rising when you fall is not for weaklings; it's for those who know they have more to offer.

Ikechi Akurunwa

CHAPTER EIGHT

THE SIXTH LAW OF FREEDOM

The sixth law of freedom: *Never stop fighting, even when everything looks hopeless.*

If you get knocked down, get up, dust yourself up and get back into the ring. Winners never stop fighting till the day they take their last breath. The fight you defer will grow taller and stronger by the time tomorrow arrives. The fight you failed to fight today will wait for you tomorrow; so, the best thing to do is pull yourself up from your bed of affliction and fight till your victory comes.

Many do not understand the bigness of their status or the importance of their roles in the sphere of human existence. Your destiny is bigger than your physical size. Your feet are bigger than the space they occupy. Your hands are strong enough to feed you and to feed a million others, so why waste such an awesome ability and responsibility by remaining on the ground of temporary defeat? Your legs have the capability to lift you up and also to lift many others. You may be the only voice that has the ability to instill hope in someone else. If that is not enough reason to get back into the ring and fight to be a vessel through which many will be blessed, I don't know what else could be.

If the prodigal son had focused on how great his fall was, he would not have had the courage to get up, let alone clawing his way back home. He overcame the pangs of hunger, he stepped over the fear of the fund to finance his journey back home, and he accepted his crazy friends in the far away land calling him chicken for planning to return to his father. He fought and won every obstacle on his way home.

There is a great reward for every sacrifice you make. You may be asking in your mind, who am I to lead a life that can affect the world? My answer to you is to simply leave that in the hands of God, the One who multiplied a few loaves of bread and scrawny fishes into huge piles, enough to feed more than five thousand people.

PHYSICAL FIGHT

The world is so good in physical fights. Humanity at large has come a long way. We have mastered the science of building bombs and mortars to wage selfish wars. We have surrounded ourselves with great castles and edifices to house our crowns and thrones.

In the medical field, some diseases that killed millions of people in the past have been eradicated or eliminated in some parts of the world. Man's progress has been phenomenal. In different spheres of life, especially in technology, man has had a lot of success. Aeronautic engineering has helped us to overcome some level of gravity. Today we can fly thousands of miles above sea level using planes and space rockets. With submarines, we can plunge into the depths of the sea and still be able to breathe, so man has found answers for so many of his physical challenges. But he has struggled with his spiritual problems since the fall of Adam. He has proven himself to be a giant in the physical arena but remains a dwarf in the spiritual realm.

SPIRITUAL FIGHT

Our fight on earth begins the day we were born. By the time we are adults, we have had many scars from different battles. It's important to know that behind most physical battles are underlying spiritual connections or triggers. And whether we win or lose largely depends on who is fighting for us in the spiritual realms.

The secret to winning spiritual fights is making sure that the God that has never lost any fight is the one fighting for you. You cannot win spiritual wars with the arm of the flesh. You cannot be a part-time Christian and win your fight with a full-time devil. Spiritual wars are spiritually won. It's a dangerous war; it's a serious war. It's a war we are engaged in every day, sometimes unaware of its ferocity.

Putting your house in order

A lot of times, we are busy fighting our external enemies instead of the more dangerous internal enemies. That's what happens when self-examination is not an important factor in shaping our lives. As we daily bury ourselves in our work, crowd our lives with programs, travel all over the world for fun, or for one event or the other, we pay less attention to the under-girding virtue of self-examination. In the quest to make it in life, we get caught up with chasing our dreams. It's easy then to brush aside the little weights that can drag us to the mud or an early grave. When we throw caution to the wind and cramp our lives with more than we can handle, we risk neglecting the most important things of life. Without self-examination, you may never realize how often you allow the little claws of carnality or the subtle hands of bad habits to strip you of your beautiful plumage or freedom. For many, it's only when the damage has been done that they suddenly realize what they have done to themselves.

Some people are afraid to confront their demons. They lack the boldness to look themselves in the mirror and tell themselves the truth about their present state. They are afraid to embark on a sincere journey of self-discovery in front of the mirror. But if you don't learn to always stop in front of the mirror, you may never see the dross buried deep in your heart or the weeds you have to cut to reap the harvest of freedom. The prodigal son's time of self-examination was a time of encounter with reality, a time of revelation, a time when God opened his eyes to see his real face. When self-examination is a daily or frequent exercise in your life, it will awaken the voice of truth that has been silenced in your conscience by the clutters in your life.

Naturally, people tend to gravitate to things with no cost attached to them or things without guardrails. Such a lifestyle can lead to habits that may never be broken. That's why we all need the guardrails of self-examination every day and every time. We need to put our house in order before the devil comes knocking.

Right weapons

Spiritual fights are more than self-examination. Among other things, it involves the use of the right weapons of defense and offense. Ephesians 6:12 says,

"For we do not wrestle against flesh and blood, but against principalities, against powers, against the rulers of the darkness of this age, against spiritual *hosts* of wickedness in the heavenly *places.*"

In view of the fact that our real battles are not physical, we have to use the right weapons to fight them. If you must win in your spiritual battles, then you have to adhere to the advice of Ephesians 6:11, which says:

"Put on the whole armor of God that you may be able to stand against the wiles of the devil."

No piece of the armors of a victorious soldier should be missing because spiritual battles are not funfairs. You must gird yourself with every needed weapon as you confront your everyday enemies. The Bible does not mince words about it. It strongly warns every soldier to properly gird themself against this onslaught.

"14Stand therefore, having girded your waist with truth, having put on the breastplate of righteousness, 15and having shod your feet with the preparation of the gospel of peace; 16above all, taking the shield of faith with which you will be able to quench all the fiery darts of the wicked

one. [17]And take the helmet of salvation, and the sword of the Spirit, which is the word of God; [18]praying always with all prayer and supplication in the Spirit, being watchful to this end with all perseverance and supplication for all the saints-" (Ephesians 6:14-18).

The helmet has saved the lives of many bikers and construction workers; the seat belt has saved the lives of many drivers and their passengers; safety glasses have saved the eyes of many welders. Gears are even more important in spiritual battles. If you are a soldier with the proper gears, you have a better chance of winning when the evil days come.

"Therefore, take up the whole armor of God that you may be able to withstand in the evil day, and having done all, to stand" (Ephesians 6:13).

Unfortunately, too many Christians are caught by the devil with no armory. Many have little or no prayer life; no quality time spent studying the Word of God; no fasted lifestyle; no time to hear from God. These are the reasons there are so many casualties because so many ignorant Christians are busy chasing miracles and shadows.

When you are well girded with the right armors, each time the devil draws close to you, he will find your heart too strong to penetrate; but if not, he'll find a heart with no door, kept open for him to enter. Without these weapons, you have no chance of living a life of freedom.

WE DON'T FIGHT ALONE

There is no reason to fight alone: most people who do have a pride problem. All you have to do in times of adversity is to reach out to people and resources available to you, and your battles will become much easier for you to win.

The love of an earthly father

It's good news to know that we don't have to fight alone in life and that there are people out there willing to help us if we humble ourselves and reach out to them. There would not have been complete victory and freedom for the prodigal son if his father didn't open his arms and his doors to him. Luke 15:20 says,

"And he arose and came to his father. But when he was still a great way off, his father saw him and had compassion, and ran and fell on his neck and kissed him."

His father never forgot his son. While the prodigal son was in a faraway land wasting his life and money, his father had him in his mind every minute of the day. He longed every day for him. He longed for the day he will see him again. Many times, he left the house, walked down to a vantage position where he could stare down the road that led to his house, hoping perhaps he might see his son heading back home. Sometimes, he probably stood there till dawn, disregarding every other thing he had planned for the day.

The prodigal son knew not how much love his father had for him. He did not know how many times his father wished he could close his eyes and open them to the sight of him returning home. He had no idea of the pain and anguish the empty space he created caused his father. He was ignorant of how many times his father ruminated over the precious times they had together or how many times he prayed to God to build a hedge of protection around his errant son or prayed for his redemption from an ungodly lifestyle.

Distance did not tamper with the love his father had for him. It reminds me of the sacrifice and risks my father undertook during the Nigerian-Biafran war for his family. Unfortunately, the war began when he was still studying in London. He worried every day about our safety. Mails were not being delivered because of the war. He couldn't reach us, and we couldn't reach him. Like the prodigal son's father, he didn't know about our condition or our whereabouts. He was troubled. He couldn't sleep at night or focus on his studies. He didn't know what to do. There were no flights from London to any part of Biafra because the British government took sides with Nigeria. When my dad couldn't take it anymore, he decided to fly to Cameroon, a neighboring country, to both Nigeria and Biafra. On getting to Cameroon, the only option he had was to risk his life through an illegal border crossing from Cameroon to Biafra; at a time, Nigerian war planes were bombing any part of Biafra they deemed fit; and their well-armed soldiers were ambushing Biafrans at the borders. It was a very dangerous journey, but he had no option. His mind was made up. He was ready to lay down his life for us. Fortunately, he made it home. With his fatherly presence and love, we were able to survive the war that took the lives of over five million Biafrans, about a third of the population of Biafra.

Do not underestimate a father's love. When the prodigal son returned home, his father was so happy that he threw a party for him.

"But the father said to his servants, 'Bring out the best robe

and put *it* on him, and put a ring on his hand and sandals on *his* feet. And bring the fatted calf here and kill *it,* and let us eat and be merry; for this, my son was dead and is alive again; he was lost and is found.'"

Luke 15:22-24

There is nothing as hard and painful as losing a child. It's something no father or mother should go through. That is why finding a lost child deserves a great celebration. The prodigal son had a great welcome party.

The love of our heavenly father

The love our heavenly father has for us is even greater. It cannot be compared to the love of an earthly father; it's immeasurable. He knows our needs and our dreams better than our earthly father. He knows the pain in our hearts and all the tears we shed over the battles we fight. He is waiting for us to come home. He is waiting for us to come running to him like the prodigal son. He is waiting for us to say,

"And the son said to him, 'Father, I have sinned against heaven and in your sight, and am no longer worthy to be called your son" (Luke 15:21).

The above plea came out of the prodigal son's mouth when he came face to face with his father. He was remorseful and repentant. Of course, his father forgave him and welcomed him back home. I would imagine all through that night he never stopped thanking God for bringing his son home safely; he never stopped thanking God for giving him the opportunity to see his son again. I would imagine the next day, he regained his lost appetite and went about the day's business with no weight on his shoulders. He probably walked around for weeks as if he had no other problem in life.

Do you know there is even greater joy in the heart of God when a sinner repents? Yes, the salvation of just one soul causes heaven to erupt with joy. Luke 15:10 says,

"Likewise, I say to you, there is joy in the presence of the angels of God over one sinner who repents."

Not only is there a party in heaven over the soul of anyone who comes running to God in repentance, but there are also the promises of great gifts greater than robes, rings and sandals that the prodigal son received immediately he got home. Luke 11:13 says,

"If you then, being evil, know how to give good gifts to your children, how much more will *your* heavenly Father give the Holy Spirit to those who ask Him!"

I Corinthians 2:9 even further expounds the incomparable and unimaginable treasures that await any prodigal son who returns to God. It says,

"But as it is written:
"Eye has not seen, nor ear heard,
Nor have entered into the heart of man
The things which God has prepared for those who love Him."

This scriptural verse above brings to light the value God places on the soul of man. It opens the curtain a little bit for us to see how important you and I are to God. There is no better place to be than the place where the presence of God abides. There is no better life to live than a redeemed life; there is no better treasure to have than a relationship with our heavenly father; there is no better hope to have than the hope of eternity in heaven where there will be no more sorrows and pain. There is nothing the world can offer you that can be more precious than God, and there is nothing too much to give up for a relationship with the God of heaven and earth, to whom the heaven and the earth belongs!

The relationship with God starts at the cross. It starts with you accepting Jesus as your Lord and personal Savior. There is no real freedom without going to the cross and availing yourself of the cleansing blood of Jesus. That is God's plan for man's redemption. No human effort or medication can substitute for the blood Jesus shed on the cross for the remission of man's sins.

Jesus is the Author of freedom, and He only can bestow it upon you.

FIGHT WITH KNOWLEDGE

Knowledge was what saved the prodigal son. He had a good knowledge of who his father was. He knew his father would welcome him back if he came begging for forgiveness. The same is true of our heavenly Father. Each time we come begging for forgiveness, He always forgives us. When the prodigal son returned home, his father completely forgave him. He embraced him with an unprecedented love. Today, many know that God is a loving Father, but they still chose to remain in captivity.

The faraway country where the prodigal son ran to can be likened to the kingdom of darkness. Armed with the knowledge of a good father, he left the place of captivity, the kingdom of darkness and returned to the place of love and forgiveness, which accurately describes the kingdom of God.

You must abhor and fight ignorance if you want to be free and remain free. Without certain knowledge, real freedom will be an illusion. Without certain knowledge, there are certain places you cannot enter, certain life-changing experiences you cannot have, and certain possessions you cannot obtain. Ignorance is a greater robber. It has robbed many of their freedom and life.

Captivity flourishes in the life of an ignorant person like cancer grows in the life of the defenseless. Any day you walk in ignorance is another day spent in one form of bondage or the other. Any day you live in ignorance is another day lived at the mercy of predators who peddle all sorts of falsehood and lies to entrap or destroy you. Any day you harbor ignorance is another day you harbored an enemy capable of enslaving and ruining your life. Freedom does not co-exist with ignorance.

Implications of ignorance

What you don't know is greater than you. If the prodigal son had a little glimpse of the hell he went through during his self-imposed exile; he wouldn't have embarked on that journey. The more you know in life, the less pain you will go through; the more you know in life, the more valuable you become to yourself, to your family and the world. Knowledge will save you time, labor, and above all, it will help you escape the chains of captivity.

Many Christians trooping in and out of churches every Sunday and Wednesday have one form of bondage or the other. Going to church is very good, but it does not exempt you from ignorance or the price of walking in it. Your prayer every day should be **"Teach me good judgment and knowledge, For I believe Your commandments"** (Psalm 119:66).

Sure, knowledge only comes from God. Job 36:12 says,

"But if they do not obey,
They shall perish by the sword,
And they shall die [a]without knowledge."

It is sad for people to live and die without the redemptive knowledge of Christ; also sad for people to live and die without the knowledge of how to walk in the freedom that Christ has obtained for humanity. It is definitely sad for people to live and die without the knowledge of their purpose and assignment on earth and to their generation.

Deadly disease

Every kind of ignorance is dangerous, but nothing is as dangerous as spiritual ignorance. Hosea 4:6 says

"My people are destroyed for lack of knowledge.
Because you have rejected knowledge,
I also will reject you from being priest for Me;
Because you have forgotten the law of your God,

I also will forget your children."

Ignorance is the most dangerous and deadly disease that can ever infect anyone: Christians or heathen, men or women; clergy or laity. Even the most educated can be the most ignorant fellow when it comes to the knowledge of God. Clergies, even, are not exempted in the abundance of ignorance in the things of God. It takes a redeemed child of God who knows how to tarry in God's presence and how to hear from God to acquire the revealed knowledge of God, which can set you free from any bondage.

Many are ignorant of their ignorance; ignorant of the consequences of living without Christ; ignorant of the dangers of playing with sin; ignorant of possessing goods that belong to Satan; ignorant of the consequences of wandering or living in the kingdom of darkness. Many Christians are ignorant of the implications of prayerlessness. They are ignorant of the dangers of not feeding their spirit daily with God's Word and of defiling their body, which is the temple of the Living God.

While ignorance is the entrance to hell's prison gates, it is the key that opens the door of poverty, sickness, blindness, defeat, and misery. To live and die without knowing how to avail oneself of the best life has to offer is a tragedy. The wise fight ignorance like a deadly disease because they know that it has the power to destroy their destiny, careers, and dreams, even their families and life. Run from ignorance; it is destructive.

Surrender the devil's goods

If you want to experience total freedom, give up the devil's goods in your hands or custody. If you don't, the devil has the legal right to hold you in captivity. The prodigal son surrendered all the goods of the foreign land. He left them in the land of his captivity. So, if you want to be free, you have to be sure you are not holding the goods of Satan. This is the reason why many prayers are not answered. It is also part of the reasons many remain sick and in bondage. Ask the Holy Spirit to reveal to you the goods of the devil in your possession or the goods of the devil you have been unknowingly peddling. As long as you have Satan's goods, he has the legal right to hold you in captivity. Proverb 22:7 says,

**"The rich rules over the poor,
And the borrower *is* servant to the lender."**

What have you borrowed from the kingdom of darkness? What do you have in your house or possession that does not glorify God? What have you borrowed from the devil to build your kingdom on the earth that may soon fade away? Give the devil back his goods today if you are serious about living a life of total freedom.

Maybe you have been under bondage for over twenty years. The good news is that no matter how deep you are in the dungeon of the devil, no matter how hooked you have become from peddling the goods of Satan, there is hope for you. God can rescue you today from the captivity of the devil and bring you into his kingdom. Colossians 1:13-14 say,

"[13]He has delivered us from the power of darkness and conveyed *us* into the kingdom of the Son of

His love,[14] in whom we have redemption through His blood, the forgiveness of sins."

This means that Jesus Christ has already paid the price for your total freedom. Once you surrender Satan's goods to him and run to Jesus, the devil will have no power or right over you again. In effect, the ball is in your court. You are the one holding yourself in captivity by refusing to let go the goods of the devil. The hands of Jesus are outstretched, waiting for you to leave your place of captivity or the kingdom of darkness and run into his waiting arms to start enjoying the freedom in the kingdom of God.

It's the knowledge or the understanding of your legal right to be free obtained by Christ that will set you free and keep you free. John 8:32 says,

"And you shall know the truth, and the truth shall make you free."

If you have been born again, what in the world are you still doing with the goods of the devil? God is a jealous God. You can't serve Him and still keep your idols. Matthew 6:24 says, **"No one can serve two masters; for either he will hate the one and love the other, or else he will be loyal to the one and despise the other. You cannot serve God and mammon."**

It's a dangerous thing to serve God and mammon. God has no patience with such people. Revelation 3:16 says, **"So then, because you are lukewarm, and neither cold nor hot, I will vomit you out of My mouth."**

Know there is power in the blood of Jesus

The blood is a powerful weapon given to the saints for their deliverance. The blood speaks for every redeemed child of God. While Abel's blood called out unto the just God for justice (Genesis 4:10), the blood of Jesus called out and is still calling out for mercy and redemption. The blood of Jesus that was shed on the cross reminds God of your redemption and your righteous standing once you have received Jesus as your Lord and Savior. The blood of Jesus reminds God of your total healing and salvation. Once God hears you pleading the blood, He knows that you understand your legal right; He sees someone standing on the legal ground granted to him or her by the shed blood of Jesus.

As an emphasis, it is important to always remember that the blood of Jesus has obtained total redemption for you and me (Ephesians 1:7); the blood of Jesus was shed at the cross at Calvary for the remission or blotting out of your sins and mine (Matthew 26:28). It's important to know that "**... according to the law almost all things are purified with blood, and without shedding of blood there is no remission**" (Hebrews 9:22).

It's important to know our victory and freedom also rest on the blood of Jesus. Revelation 12:11 testifies to this fact: **"And they overcame him by the blood of the Lamb and by the word of their testimony, and they did not love their lives to the death."**

The blood reminds the devil of his defeat, his lack of authority and right over you, the redeemed child of God. Every time you plead the blood over your life or your circumstances, you are reminding heaven of your rights and reminding the devil of his judgment and defeat. Anytime you plead the blood of Jesus, you are proclaiming to the heavens and to the kingdom of darkness that you are exercising your redemptive rights; you are reminding heaven and the devil of the finished work of Christ during which your sins, sickness, and poverty were atoned for by the blood. It is this revelation that will set you free. When you stand on this revelation and speak with knowledge and authority, the devil is obligated to let you go because he knows he has no right to hold you anymore. Anyone who knows his redemptive right and exercises it will be free and remain free.

Know there is power in the name of Jesus

Another revelation knowledge you need to stand on is the knowledge of the power and authority vested in the name of Jesus. One of the worst things that can happen to someone is to live and die without the knowledge of the inheritance that was bestowed upon him by his father. Many Africans' story is like the story of people who sat on fields of gold and gem stones without the knowledge of the wealth beneath them. They lived and died poor, blaming God for being responsible for their poverty instead of blaming their ignorance.

Unknown to many, ignorance kills faster than poverty. It has killed more people than any war or disease. It kills faster than a plague. It had sent many to the morgue before their time; robbed many of their joy and comfort; and forced many to a life of servitude and slavery. It has rendered the powerful powerless, disarmed the violent and dangerous king, subdued the proud and arrogant. Ignorance is a big burden to carry;

there is a big price to pay for ignorance. No wonder the book of Proverb 16:16 advises, **"How much better to get wisdom than gold! And to get understanding is to be chosen rather than silver."** Proverb 4:7 stresses the importance of knowledge even further. It says, **"Wisdom is the principal thing; therefore, get wisdom. And in all your getting, get understanding."**

There is a name that is higher than your problems; there is a name that is more potent and powerful than the strong arms of your captive chains, the name of Jesus.

The Bible says,
"Therefore God also has highly exalted Him and given Him the name which is above every name, that at the name of Jesus every knee should bow, of those in heaven, and of those on earth, and of those under the earth, and *that* every tongue should confess that Jesus Christ *is* Lord, to the glory of God the Father."

Philippians 2:9-11

Yes, no matter the chain that has tied you down, be it the chain of barrenness, sickness, poverty, etc., the name of Jesus has been exalted above that condition. Though this is true, but it is the revealed knowledge of this truth that will set you free and keep you free. You can recite the above scriptures as many times as you want, and nothing will happen until you come to the knowledge that there is no power of the devil, no bondage or captive chains of Satan that will not bow or surrender at the invocation of the name of Jesus Christ.

Know your kingdom legal rights

I don't want to leave you thinking that a mortal man will come to a point in his life when he will have no problems. But I want to leave you with the understanding that most of the problems human beings are carrying or tolerating have been taken care of by the redemptive work of Jesus Christ. Therefore, it will be unwise to continue to bear them day after day. If you ask people in a particular conference or church if there is anyone who does not have a problem, more than likely, no one will raise up his or her hand. However, the unfortunate thing is that most of the problems we are carrying are problems we should not be carrying. And the most significant reason behind this travesty and tragedy is ignorance, ignorance of who we are; ignorance of our rights; ignorance of our heritage, and sometimes, the ignorance of our ignorance.

Jesus came to redeem fallen man from every curse that followed him from the Garden of Eden. 1 Corinthians 15:22 says, **"For as in Adam all die, even so in Christ all shall be made alive."** Jesus had to come in human flesh in order to have the right to die so that man will live, bestowing upon humanity the legal right to demand their freedom from the devil. For the Christian to be ignorant of the rights associated with the redemptive work of grace wrought by Jesus Christ is a sad thing, a very bad place to be, and a great unnecessary burden of ignorance to bear. This lack of understanding of our redemption causes people to remain in darkness and bondage after they have been translated from the kingdom of darkness into the kingdom of light. It's like someone who was crowned a king but still lives like a commoner, someone who has been set free still living as a captive. That has been the story of many born-again Christians.

Until you understand that you can break free from your chains because Christ has broken the chains of captivity for mankind, you will continue to walk in captivity. Knowledge of your redemptive rights gives you the understanding that the curse upon your family that has not allowed any of your family members to live beyond fifty years was broken in your life the day you surrendered your life to Jesus. Without exercising your legal rights and authority as a redeemed Christian, you will die like an ordinary man or woman, and that shouldn't be so (Psalms 82:6-7).

More than ever before, this is the time to take back what belongs to you, the time to possess your possession so that you will be an asset to the kingdom of God. Enough is enough! You have suffered too long out of ignorance; it's time to rise up in faith and demand for your freedom. But you must first have a full understanding of the legal system the Christian must walk in; you must know the legal rights of a redeemed Christian. The work of redemption was built on a solid legal foundation that must be understood and exercised by every Christian who wants to be free. Some scriptures give you the legal rights to reject the attack of Satan or any affliction in your life or your family.

You should not forget that **"For this purpose, the Son of God was manifested, that He might destroy the works of the devil"** (1 John 3:8). You should not forget that **"Inasmuch then as the children have partaken of flesh and blood, He Himself likewise shared in the same, that through death He might destroy him who had the power of death, that is,** the devil..." (Hebrews 2:14). You should never forget that "Having disarmed principalities and powers, He made a public spectacle of them, triumphing over them in it" (Colossians 2:15).

These scriptures clearly highlight how God stripped every power of captivity and right from the devil. They highlight reasons why you should never be a victim or allow the devil to terrorize you. He will terrorize you if he knows you are ignorant of what you have and who you are in Christ Jesus.

Know the devil's devices

One of the devil's greatest weapons to bring into, or keep people in captivity, is the use of distraction. He distracted the prodigal son with the sight and sounds of a foreign land, and he fell for it. He distracted him with the thought of being free in a faraway land doing whatever he wants with his new found wealth, and he fell for it.

The devil wants to turn your eyes away from God and have them focused on carnal things. He wants to distract you with unimportant things to keep you away from important things like prayer or feeding your spirit with the Word of God. He wants you to focus on the size of your mountain instead of on the size of your God. At one time, Peter, heeding the call of Jesus, stepped out of a boat and walked on water. But the moment the devil distracted Peter, and he turned his eyes away from Jesus unto the colossal waves surrounding him, Peter began to sink!

The Bible records this incident in Matthew 14:28-30 as

follows:

"[28]And Peter answered Him and said, "Lord, if it is You, command me to come to You on the water." [29]So He said, "Come." And when Peter had come down out of the boat, he walked on the water to go to Jesus. [30]But when he saw [a]that the wind *was* boisterous, he was afraid; and beginning to sink, he cried out, saying, "Lord, save me!"

To be ignorant of the devices of the devil can leave you perpetually in bondage. Distraction is an old weapon of the devil, and he does a good job with it. 2 Corinthians 2:11 says, **"... lest Satan should take advantage of us; for we are not ignorant of his devices."** It is clear that ignorance can turn you into a toy that the devil can play with anyhow he likes. Every day a lot of lives are ruined by ignorance. Every day most prayers are not answered due to ignorance. Every day most greatness and talents are killed by ignorance.

Knowledge without action

Knowledge is power, but knowledge without corresponding action or response is useless. Ignorance is not only the absence of knowledge; it's also the absence of the right action or response after knowledge is acquired. The prodigal son would have died in captivity in a foreign land if he had not taken the action to return to his father. When you take the right action, you will have the right result. In one of my poems, I wrote:

This stump will rise,
this stump of the felled tree,
will rise again.

Though dusts and ashes gather
to build their vile altars on it,
yet this stump will rise again.

Though cluster flies aggregate daily
to wipe their dirty mouth and feet on it,
yet this stump will rise again.

Though Bark and Button spiders
fight to erect their gallows around its edges,
yet this stump will rise again.

From every straddle and every saddle
holding it down,
this stump will rise again.
From every smoke and every murk,
hiding its face,
this stump will rise again.

From every rubble and every stubble
building a tomb over it,
this stump will rise again.

For unbeknown to everyone,
it has been slowly growing new roots downward
and a new shoot upward,

and soon,
all that have written it off,
will see it rise again.

Take action about your life today. James 2:26 says, **"For as the body without the spirit is dead, so faith without works is dead also."**

Food for thoughts

- With deep roots, it will be hard for any wind of adversity to uproot you. You are as strong as the depth of your roots. Deepen your roots every day, and you will deepen your joy and peace of mind. Deepen your roots, and your freedom will be strongly anchored.

- Nothing can defeat a man who sets his eyes on the finish line and not on the mountains ahead of him.

- If you keep moving, you have a better chance of crossing the finish line than someone who has made his bed at the foot of his mountain.

- Your actions or inaction in the face of a problem is a measure of your inner strength. Your inner strength defines who you are and how far you can go in life.

- Those you consider your antagonists are only irons meant to smoothen your rough edges. If you know how to seize those moments, you will live to be a shining star.

CHAPTER NINE

THE SEVENTH LAW OF FREEDOM

The seventh law of freedom: *The longer you stay in the presence of God in the morning, the safer you become the rest of the day.*

Have you acquired something precious but lost it a few months later? I have. Years ago, before my wedding, I bought a beautiful wedding ring for my fiancée from London. I was very proud of myself for hunting down such a gorgeous piece of gold for her. She adored it. It was precious to her. But one day, shortly after our wedding, she took it off her finger and carefully placed it on the edge of the bathtub. Unfortunately, it slid and fell into the bathtub drain and disappeared. It was painful. It happened over twenty-eight years ago, but it's still fresh in my mind because we lost something precious to us. The irony of life is that most times, after losing something of value, we resort to blaming ourselves or someone else. Some would say, "Why am I so careless?" Or "Why is it that everything I touch vanishes or falls apart?" The right question should be, "What can I do to avoid making such mistakes again?"

After giving your life to Christ or running back to God as the prodigal son did, the question you should ask yourself is, "What can I do to avoid slipping back to my old life or making the old mistakes again?" Or, "What can I do to remain faithful to God day after day?" Paul was so confident of his testimony that towards the end of his earthly journey, he boldly declared,

"I have fought the good fight, I have finished the race, I have kept the faith..." (2 Timothy 4:7).

You cannot afford to place your gold ring on a slippery surface as my wife did; if you do, it may slide down and disappear into the drain. Your life is worth protecting. Your Christian faith is more precious than jewelry, so make sure you plant your feet on the solid Rock, not on the world's shifting sand.

After the glorious reunion and restoration, the prodigal son did not run away from home again! He completely turned away from the temporary pleasures of this world. He remained in the presence of his father, where counsel and guidance were abundant. As long as he stayed home, he had food and safety. As long as he remained in his father's presence, he never lacked fatherly love and care.

Where are you?

Where are you? This was the question God asked Adam in the Garden of Eden.

"Then the LORD God called to Adam and said to him,

"Where are you? So, he said, "I heard Your voice in the garden, and I was afraid because I was naked; and I hid myself," (Genesis 3:9).

After Adam disobeyed God by eating the forbidden fruit in the middle of the garden with Eve, he started hiding. Once he disobeyed God by not heeding to God's instruction, he lost the provision and protection of God. Instead of enjoying the abundant life of the Garden of Eden, now he has to labor to provide for himself. Instead of enjoying divine covering, he had to make leaves to cover himself (Genesis 3:17-19).

From the above scriptures, it's obvious that sin keeps us away from the presence of God. Sin makes us to hide from God. What a loss for Adam and the rest of humanity! He sacrificed fellowship and the blessings of God for the temporary pleasure of satisfying his taste bud. He sacrificed the daily fellowship with God, the wonderful and glorious experience to be in the presence of God for a moment of pleasure. What a loss!

The story is the same today wherever you go. The church is full of pleasure seekers instead of God-seekers, fun lovers instead of God lovers, and excitement hunters instead of God hunters. Instead of Spirit-filled Christians, the church is full of casual or part-time Christians with one leg in the church and one leg in the world. The church has become a place for entertainment and socialization, instead of being a place of worshipping God in truth and in spirit. We have turned the house of God into a business arena where we exchange money and pleasantries. No wonder God is hardly present in our churches today. It's unimaginable what the church has lost, what she has sacrificed for the pleasures of the world. It's inconceivable how the church has failed God because of the pursuit of money, fame and power. The church today can hardly stay away from the likes of the forbidden fruit.

We lose so much by not staying in the presence of God. The girlfriend robbing you of your fellowship with God is not worth going to hell for, neither the few minutes of pleasure with pornography worth substituting for the sweet presence of God. That job that gives you the opportunity to steal money, like most politicians in Africa, is not worth substituting for eternal damnation. Nothing is worth substituting for the sweet presence of God and what He has in store for humanity in heaven.

The serious-minded Christians are found more in the secret place where they spend time with God than in the presence of men. While others are glued to the TV, they are glued on their knees in the presence of God; while others are busy counting their silvers and gold, they are busy crying for the souls of sinners. Many so-called Christians are in the presence of men seeking praises and accolades, while the serious-minded Christians are in the presence of God surrendering their soul, spirit and body to Him.

What are you doing?

What are you doing? Is the pursuit of silver and gold more important to you than the kingdom business? Jesus once responded to a question by saying,

"Why did you seek Me? Did you not know that I must be about My Father's business?" (Luke 2:49)

How much time do you invest in building the kingdom of God? How much money do you invest in building the kingdom of God? Please, do not mistake building the kingdom of God for building a ministry or church, for a pastor who sees or runs a church as a personal or family business. Beloved, consider giving only to churches surrendered to God and not to those in the clutches of one man or a family.

When you invest in people around you who have needs, especially those of the household of God, you are also building the kingdom of God. Too many African Christians are neglecting this part of their assignment and are losing the reward of being their brother's keeper. Most times, we neglect the widows, the homeless, the jobless, and the hungry. We bypass them as we go to church, where we, most times, empty our pockets. There is a great reward for taking care of the poor among us. It's a great ministry. But how can you give to the poor around you when every week you empty your pocket in your church? You should give to the church but don't forget the poor around you. Your money is not for the church alone. God has a special reward for those who, before they empty their pockets in their churches, make provision for the widows and orphans in their midst.

"³⁴Then the King will say to those on His right hand, 'Come, you blessed of My Father, inherit the kingdom prepared for you from the foundation of the world: ³⁵for I was hungry and you gave Me food; I was thirsty and you gave Me drink; I was a stranger and you took Me in; ³⁶I *was* naked and you clothed Me; I was sick and you visited Me; I was in prison and you came to Me.'

"³⁷Then the righteous will answer Him, saying, 'Lord, when did we see You hungry and feed *You,* or thirsty and give *You* drink? ³⁸When did we see You a stranger and take *You* in, or naked and clothe *You?* ³⁹Or when did we see You sick, or in prison, and come to You?' ⁴⁰And the King will answer and say to them, 'Assuredly, I say to you, inasmuch as you did *it* to one of the least of these My brethren, you did *it* to Me.'"

Matthew 25:34-40

Never, never schedule your giving and leave out your needy neighbors, widows, and orphans; even strangers. But to accomplish this, you have to be careful with being brainwashed by pastors that milk believers of their hard-earned money to feed their flamboyant lifestyles. You have to be careful with churches where every church member comes to church only to build the kingdom of one man, the pastor! The church should be a place where a pastor helps every member fulfill the purpose for which God created them, not a place where every other person's ministry, but the pastor's, is hijacked.

You can lay a good giving foundation with this scripture:

"**When you have finished laying aside all the tithe of your increase in the third year—the year of tithing—and have given** *it* to the *Levite, the stranger, the fatherless, and the widow,* **so that they may eat within your gates and be filled, then you shall say before the LORD your God: 'I have removed the holy** *tithe* **from** *my* **house, and also have given them to the Levite, the stranger, the fatherless, and the widow, according to all Your commandments which**

You have commanded me; I have not transgressed Your commandments, nor have I forgotten *them.*"
Deuteronomy 26:12-13

The above scriptural verses clearly underscore the fact that, in your giving, you must never exclude strangers, the fatherless and the widows. Again, never ever schedule your giving and leave out the widows, orphans and strangers around you.

And in all your giving or services, do not fail to give all the glory to God. Whatever seed God leads you to plant on a fertile ground for the building of His kingdom, give all the glory to Him. Remember Isaiah 42:8 says,

**"I *am* the LORD, that *is* My name;
And My glory I will not give to another,
Nor My praise to carved images."**

If your lifestyle is contrary to the life of Christ, probably you have been spending little or no time alone with God, reconsider your habits today. If you stay long enough in the presence of God, you will learn his ways. You will give like Him, talk like Him, walk like Him, love like Him, and think like Him. A life that has not been laid on the altar of sacrifice so that God will transform and mold it into a vessel He can use will likely be marked by carnality and ruled by the flesh. Unfortunately, too many Christians are unwilling to pay the price for being Christ-like or make the necessary sacrifice needed to empty themselves completely so that God can fill them with His power and unction. Many are not willing to crucify their flesh through prayer so that they can be alive in the spirit. God is waiting for you to be that willing and surrendered vessel.

Who are you working for?

There is always the temptation to say to others what you heard from your flesh or what your ego wants you to say instead of what God said. There is also the temptation to build your ministry in your own way and not in the way God demands of you. Jonah is a good example.

> "¹Now the word of the LORD came to Jonah the son of Amittai, saying, '²Arise, go to Nineveh, that great city, and cry out against it; for their wickedness has come up before Me.' ³But Jonah arose to flee to Tarshish from the presence of the LORD. He went down to Joppa, and found a ship going to Tarshish; so, he paid the fare, and went down into it, to go with them to Tarshish from the presence of the LORD."
>
> Jonah 1:1-3

God gave Jonah a message to deliver to the people of Nineveh; instead of going to Nineveh and declaring to them the message God had for them, he decided to go to Tarshish! God sent him to a particular city for a particular assignment; he decided to go to another city of his own accord.

Who are you working for? The ministry you are setting up in Tarshish, is it because the city of Tarshish is more developed than the city of Nineveh and would attract wealthier people to your church? That very missionary offering you are raising this month, is it to further the Gospel or to set up a side business? Too many people start well in ministry, but as soon as their ministries grow, they become distracted by money, power and human worship. There are those who, at the beginning, never did anything unless they heard from God, but after a while, they began to copy what other pastors are doing, and before they knew it, they had abandoned the altar where they heard from God for the altar of worldly glory. That's a dangerous thing to do. Stay in your assignment. Do God's bidding, not the bidding of men or the flesh. It's a costly and dangerous thing to do.

Your decision to go to Tarshish against God's instruction can cause problem for innocent people helping you to build your kingdom in the wrong city. Jonah's disobedience caused a lot of problems to the people in the ship he boarded en route to Tarshish. During the journey, God sent a storm to trouble the ship. When things became bad, some people in the boat, possibly traders, sacrificed their goods by throwing them into the sea to make the ship lighter and safer. They suffered a great loss because of rebellious Jonah. And until he was thrown overboard, the storm did not stop. The travelers would have lost their lives because of the disobedience of Jonah.

"⁴But the LORD sent out a great wind on the sea, and there was a mighty tempest on the sea, so that the ship was about to be broken up. ⁵Then the mariners were afraid; and every man cried out to his god, and threw the cargo that *was* in the ship into the sea, to lighten the load. But Jonah had gone down into the lowest parts of the ship, had lain down, and was fast asleep."

Jonah 1:4-5

The times we live in are dangerous times. It's not the time to board the wrong ship; it's not the time to head in the wrong direction or to the wrong city to do your own bidding. Who are you working for? Why are you in ministry? Why are you a worker in the church? Are you working for personal gain? Were you attracted to ministry all because you love the idea of someone calling you 'Daddy' or 'Mummy' and literally bowing to you every time they see you? Who really are you working for? If you are working for God, by all means, step aside and let God run His church! Discard your huge ego and greed, crucify your flesh, and let God have His way in your life and ministry.

The safest place

After you have come to the knowledge of your legal redemption rights, then kneel before God in brokenness and make your petitions and your case known to God, and heaven will open for you. As you tarry in the presence of God and plead your case before Him, your freedom will come. There is no yoke that cannot fall off in the presence of God from the life of a saint who knows his right and how to plead his case with a broken spirit. In the presence of God, there is a yoke-breaking anointing; in the presence of God, there is power able to transport you from prison to a high throne of authority like Joseph (Genesis 41:14). In the presence of God, there is an anointing for healing and deliverance! In the presence of God, there is enough fire to refine you into a holy vessel, as well as enough power to deliver total freedom to you.

The secret to total and complete freedom lies in knowing your redemptive legal rights and kneeling in God's presence constantly until your freedom comes. How much time do you spend in God's presence each day? How much time do you spend talking to your heavenly Father, bringing your petitions to Him and making your case before Him? If you know how to spend time in the presence of God and how to exercise your redemptive rights, you will constantly walk in freedom. Every day, as you rise from your knees, you will carry His presence with you to anywhere you go; the world will run to you to know your secret or to seek answers for their problems.

God's presence is more important than having a ministry. Abandoning your altar of prayer will, in the end, lead to the spiritual decay of your life and ministry. No man or pastor will ever reveal to you what God will disclose to you in your closet; no man will speak to you better than God when you spend time in His presence. There are secrets only God can tell you in your secret place. Kneel in His presence until He speaks.

Men and women who cannot hear from God are of little value to the world in need of a Savior. Kneeling unlocks prison doors for you and for the rest of the world. His presence is the only safe place; it's the only place where Freedom is guaranteed. Never forget that the longer you stay in the presence of God in the morning, the safer it becomes for you the rest of the day. The less you stay in God's presence, the more impoverished you will become. The less you stay in the presence of God, the less powerful you will become. The less you stay in the presence of God, the less free you become.

Food for thoughts

- Freedom is a byproduct of diligence, as affirmed by

Proverb 22:29, which says, **"Do you see a man *who* excels in his work? He will stand before kings; He will not stand before unknown *men.*"** Having the freedom to associate with kings does not come cheap.

- The very presence of God is the only safe place. Indeed, nowhere is safer than the presence of the Almighty and all-powerful God.

- The presence of God is the only place Freedom is guaranteed. You can't constantly tarry in the presence of the Author of freedom and not be free. If you clothe yourself with God's abiding presence and glory, you will inevitably be clothed with His abiding freedom and power.

- To the level you know how to walk with God is to the level, you will be free and remain free.

CHAPTER TEN

THE EIGHTH LAW OF FREEDOM

The eighth law of freedom: *To the degree you value your freedom is to the degree you will be free.*

If you ask the prodigal son the worth of his freedom a few days after he returned to the loving arms of his father, he would likely tell you that it was worth everything to him. Indeed, freedom is worth everything. It could determine how far you would go in life. It could also be an important factor in deciding what could be entrusted to you or who would be allowed to be around you. To be a serious-minded Christian or achiever, being free must be of utmost importance to you at all times.

There was a time bush-lamp was gold. It meant everything to a villager because of the usual lack of electricity in villages. Those days, each time you have to walk through any narrow and scary village path at night, you held your lamp firmly in your hand and tried as much as you can to guard its light from dying on you because your freedom, safety, and peace of mind depended on it. In the same vein, freedom plays a major role in your peace of mind and success in life as you journey through the dark world of today. And you're being free and staying free, in turn, depend on what priority you place on things that would guarantee your freedom.

You are born a hero

Maybe you don't know you are born a hero. This truth is most often not realized by many. Everyone is born with greatness engraved on their forehead, but many never achieve greatness because their destinies were hijacked by captivity in one area or another of their lives.

It should be pointed out that captivity includes things most people often don't consider as captivity, like ignorance, habits of procrastination, excessive love for food and sleep. Most people are only familiar with things like being shackled in jail or being a drug addict. Anything that hinders you from moving forward at the right speed is a form of captivity.

Be watchful every day because the Devil is a master planner. He knows most people are as strong as their weakest point, so he fights day and night in our areas of weakness until he imprisons those he can. So, the reason most people die without tasting greatness is not that they were born failures. Rather, they were denied freedom in one area of their lives and therefore defeated through their most vulnerable area. If you visit the prison, you will see the world's best talented and gifted people languishing in jail after falling to one weakness or the other. Always remember you are as strong as your weakest point. A rope will always snap from its weakest point. A wall will always cave in first from its weakest point. If you want to remain a hero, you must not allow any weakness or weak point to thrive in your life for a long time.

The good news is that there are stories of people who overcame addiction or freed themselves from chains of captivity to climb to the top of the ladder of life. Their stories serve as a testament to the fact that you can be free today and go on to become successful in life. Many books have been written by people who overcame one addiction or another to rise to prominence. I recommend such books for anyone whose destiny has been hijacked by one little habit or addiction. Books like *From Prison to Praise* and *From Crack Addict to CEO* are stories of great men whose lives were interrupted for years by addiction.

God's plan

From creation, God's perfect will for man is a life of freedom; that was what Adam and Eve had
in the Garden of Eden before the devil stripped it from them. In Eden, God came down to have fellowship with them constantly. They were free and enjoyed this amazing garden that had everything they needed. They had wonderful times with God as long as they stayed away from the fruit God told them not to eat. The very day they ate the forbidden fruit, they lost their freedom, and their lives began to fall apart.

Genesis 3: 3 says, **"...but of the fruit of the tree which *is* in the midst of the garden, God has said, 'You shall not eat it, nor shall you touch it, lest you die.'"**

Forbidden fruit is anything offensive to God, anything God

wants a Christian or any other human being to stay away from. As long as the Christian keeps away from things offensive to God, he will have the freedom and privilege of constantly fellowshipping with Him. Such a Christian will have the freedom to constantly enjoy God's wonderful presence and glory; he will have constant access to God's Throne Room where divine mysteries are unveiled. Also, he will have access to other kingdom blessings not available to people who walk in disobedience.

For Adam and Eve, the forbidden fruit was worth more than their freedom and fellowship with God by their actions. How much is your freedom worth to you? Maybe a five minutes kiss with Jezebel is worth more to you than your soul? Maybe a two-minute thrill with pornography is worth more to you than your soul? Maybe a car is worth more to you than your freedom because you are willing to do anything to buy the car of your dream? Maybe a house is worth more than your freedom because you are willing to sell your soul to make money to buy your dream home. Maybe a job is worth more than your freedom as you are willing to embark on any compromise to get a job. Some of the things people sacrifice for their freedom are unthinkable. Many people fight, lie, cheat, steal and do so many disgraceful things just to have perishable goods, forfeiting their precious relationship with the Almighty God and His imperishable treasures.

The everyday test

There are Christians who carry big Bibles and sing the loudest who have lost their freedom and fellowship with God and are just pretending to be spiritually alive. Deep down in their hearts, they know they are not what they portray. But because they want to be successful by any means necessary, they continue the path of constant life of compromise, lust, the pursuit of self-glory, self-gratification and other destructive lifestyles and appetites, covering their false lives with the shining robe of hypocrisy.

Every day, the devil presents the forbidden fruit to all of us; the forbidden fruit of fornication, the forbidden fruit of adultery, stealing, pride, and other vices. How do you respond to these laced and glamorized offers or opportunities to sin? Are you one of those who, after eating the forbidden fruit, find someone else to give the fruit to eat? Do you go about quoting one of the greatest lies of the devil, "We are all sinners," to justify your sinful actions? How can every Christian be a sinner after they have been saved from sin? If indeed we are all sinners after salvation, then Christ died in vain. Many agents of the devil and even some ignorant Christians deliberately go about spreading the plague of sin to others by convincing them just to take a little bite of the forbidden fruit. They say, "It's just a little kiss, or a little sin, or a little compromise. It won't hurt that much after all." Please run from such people. Avoid them like the plague, and if possible, 'unfriend' them on your social media platforms. Keep a good distance from them! Such relationships do not compare with the joy of fellowshipping with God or walking in the freedom that comes only by refusing to eat the forbidden fruit of sin and death.

It's important to note that apart from losing your freedom, anytime you eat the forbidden fruit, it gives the devil the opportunity or license to attack you. This is how most people open the door of their lives to all sorts of afflictions and demonic powers. Sin separates us from God, and once Satan sees the separation, he seizes the opportunity and ruthlessly strikes. Before you realize what happened, you have become trapped and taken captive by the devil.

Stay away from anything that will separate you from God! Stay away from anything the Bible has warned you to desist from, and you will be in constant fellowship with God. You will constantly walk in His presence and enjoy the blessings of tarrying in His presence. Don't play with sin and think you will ever experience the joy of living and walking in freedom. Anytime you willfully sin, you are willfully walking away from God's territory of protection into the dangerous territory of Satan. There are grave consequences for such reckless behavior. When you wander into the enemy's territory in search of his goods, he may take you captive. He is good at throwing anything he can lay his hands on at people to weaken them and make them easy preys.

Don't toy with your freedom by toying with forbidden fruits. It could cost you your life. It cost Samson his life; it cost Saul his throne; it cost Judas his soul. Yes, toying with sin cost Jonah his dignity and three days of captivity in the belly of a fish! It cost Ananias and Sapphira their lives, and it turned Lot's wife into a pillar of salt. The list is endless.

After they ate the forbidden fruit, what followed Adam and Eve was a litany of curses and sorrows that rolled over to the rest of humanity. Be careful how you live your life. Don't compromise your faith and trivialize your salvation, or you may end up sacrificing your freedom. Don't live your life to please other people rather than God, or you may end up sacrificing your freedom. Don't settle for easy money, an easy lifestyle and an easy way out of things that need to be properly addressed, or it may cost you your freedom.

The question you must answer

What is freedom worth to you? Is your freedom worth more than a little pleasure? Is your freedom worth more than a little moment of earthly glory? Is your freedom worth more than a little pride and applause of men? Is your freedom worth more than the perishable things the world offers?

Your freedom is in your hands. If you trade it for worthless things, you will definitely pay a costly price. If you value it, you will protect it at all cost. In life, you will hardly retain anything you don't value. To the degree you value, your freedom is to the degree you will be free. God wants you free, and you can be free and remain free by living according to the tenets of the cardinal laws of freedom.

Food for thoughts

- A rope will always snap from its weakest point. A wall will always cave in first from its weakest point.

- Freedom is not the right to do whatever you want, but the will and the power to do what is right.

- When two powers clash, the superior power will always win. Make sure you have the backing of the superior power of God in your daily fights, and your victory and freedom in life will be guaranteed.

PRAYER OF SALVATION

If you would like to accept Jesus as your personal Lord and Savior, pray this simple prayer by faith, and you will become a born-again child of God.

"Dear God, thank you for sending your Son to die on the cross for my sins. According to Your Word, if I acknowledge that You raised Jesus from the dead and that I accept Him as my Lord and Savior, I would be saved. Right now, I forsake my sins, and I accept Jesus as my personal Lord and Savior. Thank you for hearing my prayers, and forgiving my sins and giving me a brand-new life. I confess and believe that from today, Jesus is my Lord and my Savior."

Congratulations! Welcome to the family of God's redeemed people. Join a church or a Christian fellowship to help you grow and mature in the Lord.

www.ingramcontent.com/pod-product-compliance
Lightning Source LLC
Chambersburg PA
CBHW031556040426
42452CB00006B/326